teach yourself

the internet for writers

john ralph

The **teach yourself** series does exactly what it says, and it works. For over 60 years, more than 40 million people have learnt over 750 subjects the **teach yourself** way, with impressive results.

be where you want to be
with **teach yourself**

For UK orders: please contact Bookpoint Ltd., 130 Milton Park, Abingdon, Oxon OX14 4SB. Telephone: +44 (0)/1235 827720. Fax: +44 (0)/1235 400454. Lines are open 09.00–18.00, Monday to Saturday, with a 24-hour message answering service. You can also order through our website www.teachyourself.co.uk.

For USA order enquiries: please contact McGraw-Hill Customer Services, PO Box 545, Blacklick, OH 43004-0545, USA. Telephone: 1-800-722-4726. Fax: 1-614-755-5645.

For Canada order enquiries: please contact McGraw-Hill Ryerson Ltd., 300 Water St, Whitby, Ontario L1N 9B6, Canada. Telephone: 905 430 5000. Fax: 905 430 5020.

Long renowned as the authoritative source for self-guided learning – with more than 40 million copies sold worldwide – the *Teach Yourself* series includes over 300 titles in the fields of languages, crafts, hobbies, business, computing and education.

British Library Cataloguing in Publication Data
A catalogue record for this title is available from The British Library.

Library of Congress Catalog Card Number: On file.

First published in UK 2003 by Hodder Headline Plc., 338 Euston Road, London, NW1 3BH.

First published in US 2003 by Contemporary Books, A Division of The McGraw-Hill Companies, 1 Prudential Plaza, 130 East Randolph Street, Chicago, Illinois 60601 USA.

The 'Teach Yourself' name is a registered trade mark of Hodder & Stoughton Ltd.

Copyright © 1996, 1998, 2003 John Ralph

Typeset by MacDesign, Southampton
Printed in Great Britain for Hodder & Stoughton Educational, a division of Hodder Headline Plc, 338 Euston Road, London NW1 3BH by Cox & Wyman Ltd., Reading, Berkshire.

Papers used in this book are natural, renewable and recyclable products. They are made from wood grown in sustainable forests. The logging and manufacturing processes conform to the environmental regulations of the country of origin.

Impression number   10 9 8 7 6 5 4 3 2 1

Year   2007 2006 2005 2004 2003

contents

acknowledgements

My thanks go to Allen Rolf (1934–2000), who first stimulated my interest in the Web as a source for writing research and handed out invaluable advice to me and to anyone in need; to Bob Faw for US details where, if anything is wrong, it is down to my misunderstanding and not his facts; to all the C-Hers for their unstinting help and encouragement; to everyone who so readily gave their permission for quotes. And of course Elisabeth, for her love and support in good times and bad.

Conventions used

When you see something that needs to be typed into your computer, such as:

'subscribe inklings <yourname@youraddress>'

the quotation marks are not entered. Text within the <caret marks> should be changed to your own details – **bgates@microsoft.com** if you happen to be that particular billionaire – and the caret marks are not entered.

When you see an address ending in a period or full stop do not enter it. It is just there for punctuation in the text. A dot in an address implies that something should be to the right of it, thus **www.microsoft.com** is a valid address, but entering **www.microsoft.com.** might not work as your browser would be expecting another part of the address after **com**.

preface

When I first connected to the Internet the Web was in its infancy. Programs were used under DOS on the PC and TELNET connections were common. A good graphic was one made from ASCII code – letters that turned into a picture if you screwed your eyes up real tight and used your imagination a lot. I had to learn the subset of Unix that was used as well as all the necessary DOS commands and was never comfortable with it all.

The connected world was also full of capitalized acronyms. I hated those.

The world is growing up. It is no longer the sole preserve of 'anoraks' and mystical bearded programmers who live on caffeine and pizza. We mortals are allowed in as well and have the use of easy to understand (or so it says in the instruction manual) graphical interfaces and many kind people have hacked code to make life a lot simpler for us and a lot more colourful. There is still a lot to learn though, with URLs, FTP and HTML, and the learning process can be, if not painful, a little fraught. And the world is *still* full of capitalized acronyms. And I *still* hate them.

My aim in writing this book has been to hand over some of the tips and information that I have gleaned over the last few years from my own efforts and from learning through the efforts of others. May it make your discovery of the Internet and what it can do for you as a writer a little more enjoyable than it might otherwise have been.

I hope that you enjoy the book and even more that you enjoy the Internet. It's big. Really big. In fact it's bigger than you can possibly imagine. Even if you screw your eyes up real tight!

John Ralph
Henley-on-Thames
January 2003

What a writer gains from the Internet

The press refer to it as 'the Information Superhighway'. Conversations at dinner parties now revolve around it. Addresses for it appear on business cards. Companies are falling over themselves to be represented on it. Vast quantities of money are being made and lost on it every day.

Created as a network for the US armed forces and for easy connection between academic centres, and designed to give continuous communication in the event of nuclear war, the Internet has become the recent focus of a great deal of attention by those in-the-know and also those who only think they are in-the-know. Why should you, as a writer, be at all interested in it? Because, like it or not, it is probably going to change your writing life.

The Internet is widely used for sending e-mail. If you have not been connected yourself, but have just talked to those who are connected, you may be forgiven for thinking that it is used for little else; indeed, many people are quite satisfied with limiting themselves to just that use. If e-mail were all it offered it would be of little interest to writers beyond being a neat form of communication, a new way of doing what writers have always done – some more successfully than others. It is, in fact, a great deal more than a system for cheap and rapid letter writing; it is a change of paradigm for the writer's world.

If you are an aspiring writer needing advice on how to get your dialogue just right, there is exactly that kind of advice out there. If you feel that you have not quite got the hang of formatting a script for your latest film idea, the Internet is the place to go for help. Your novel is set in Los Angeles and you are not sure if your protagonist can physically get from one spot to another in the way you want? There are street maps of major US cities. You need background material for that article on genetic engineering you want to write? Look no further than the Internet. Searching for a quote? It is there, somewhere. Do you want to – publish a book? – find guidelines to write an article for a magazine? – know if an agent you might like to use is bona fide? Yes, it *is* on the Net.

The computer press has an overworked phrase: 'all human knowledge is out there'. It is becoming closer to the truth as time goes by and the Internet matures. Much of the help you might need as a writer is on the Internet somewhere, waiting to be found.

What the Internet is

Reading the popular press you would be forgiven for thinking that the Internet was just the World Wide Web (Web or WWW). While the Web is now arguably the major part of it and is most easily and frequently accessed, there is a great deal more. The older part of the Internet is still there, its text-oriented nature and its Unix computer language flavour showing its age and pedigree.

Recent programs, written mostly as add-ons for other Internet packages, take away much of the complex and sometimes arcane language needed in the past to communicate across the vast network of computers that is the Internet. Transfer of files using File Transfer Protocol (FTP) can be easily carried out now using familiar 'point-and-click' or 'drag-and-drop' techniques under Windows on a PC and using similar techniques on a Mac. Access to e-mail and newsgroups is simple using any one of dozens of proprietary programs. The newer Web is easily visited with browser software such as Netscape's Navigator or Microsoft's Internet Explorer, which also link to e-mail and newsgroup access. The Web and the browsers also allow file transfers with no knowledge of FTP and directory structures needed at all. Indeed, if you restrict your Internet use to the Web, some of what you are reading in this introduction will come under the heading of 'nice to know' rather than 'need to know'. Restrict yourself in this way, however, and you will cut yourself off from a wealth of information. If you intend to use the Internet to full and best advantage some background knowledge will help.

Internet use spread from the US military, first across academic communities worldwide, then the computer 'geek' population. E-mail allowed easy personal communication; newsgroups gave voices to parties with similar interests. Internet Relay Chat (IRC) gave almost instant, multi-way conference facilities; FTP enabled the transfer of programs and data files from one remote computer to another; TELNET enabled users to access remote computers and use them as if they were on a desk in front of them.

These abilities were more or less restricted to computer near-experts. The programs used were far from user friendly, the language needed was esoteric and the end results were not always what was expected. A new system was devised that used HyperText Markup Language (HTML). This was originally designed for workers at CERN to enable them to easily access the new information pouring out daily from laboratories and research institutes. Within pages of text, references to other – relevant – texts were highlighted and marked with hidden codes; a simple mouse click on the highlighted text took the user to another page of text – not necessarily in the same document. This enabled a reader to jump from one place to another easily and in a logical manner, linking different texts together, enabling cross-references to be navigated and facilitating return to the original document if and when desired. Further developments of the HTML language and the wide introduction of browser programs gave rise to the Web of today, where pages of text and graphics are stored on the Internet and cross-referenced to each other by links.

Once you are connected to the Internet you have immediate access to millions of other computers worldwide, all at the same time and usually only a local phone call away. On these computers are billions of Web pages, millions of gigabytes of data and several million users. The knowledge of the world is yours.

What this book is not

The Internet is similar in many respects to a living organism. It displays organic properties in that it changes and grows all the time. Never standing still, it is hard to pin down and describe in a way that will be as valid tomorrow as it is today.

There are many books that offer long lists of Internet addresses and even longer descriptions of what may be found at these sites. Their usefulness is limited. An address that is valid today may tomorrow lead to a dead site; a link referred to in a book may just not function properly when the reader tries it. The Internet is dynamic; its immediacy does not lend itself to printed text. What you will not find, therefore, within these pages is a hold-your-hand guide-to-software and a list of sites of possible interest. There are addresses given – plenty of them scattered through the text and some long lists gathered and sorted in appendices – but there can be no guarantee that they will all work properly by the time you read this book even though care has been taken in their selection for inclusion and they were all checked for validity just before publication. A different approach has been made in order, hopefully, to increase the time that the book will stay relevant to the real and changing world.

Several attempts have been made at taming the vast confusion of data on the Internet, some more successful than others. Different approaches have led to different solutions, each with their own idiosyncratic results. This book aims to describe in general terms what benefits there might be for writers to be connected to the Internet. It hopes to delineate strategies which can be used to get the best value from being connected and to show how a writer can get the information he or she needs from the morass of information out there. It explains what other writers on the Internet can do for you and how they can help, support and guide you in your writing quests. It does not set out to be a concordance for the Internet or even a partial index to it, rather it sets out to explain how to use the indexes which are on the Net already, giving tips on what to look for when searching for specific topics or researching broader backgrounds.

The content of these indexes, or search engines, is dynamic and changes from day to day. If these regularly updated indexes can lead to broken links and pages that do not exist any more or have moved – and believe me they can – a printed book has little chance of being up to date with the exact locations of pages or files. All is not lost, however; there are techniques that can be used to track down that elusive page that someone mentioned was well worth looking at. You will find some of them here.

There are many new technologies on the Internet and also some new ways to do old things. Many of these have been given strange names that might be unfamiliar to you. At the back of this book, therefore, there is a glossary explaining terms that you might not recognize; so if you do not understand a term or expression this should be your first port of call.

01

overview of the internet

In this chapter you will learn

- how newsgroups work
- the basics of the World Wide Web
- how to join communities and mailing lists

This chapter is meant to give a very quick description of what is out there on the Internet. If you have been using the Net for some time, then you can probably skip this chapter. However, even a long-time user may not have run across some of the resources available and might find it beneficial to skim it.

The chapter does not mean to supplant the Help files associated with any program you may be using such as Internet Explorer, Outlook, Turnpike, Eudora or any of the dozens of Net-related products available. On the contrary, you are positively encouraged to read those Help files. It is intended to give an overview of parts of the Internet that could be of use to a writer, so that the following chapters, which explore the resources in a little more depth, can be read without continual breaks for explanations of the basics.

1.1 Newsgroups

What a newsgroup is

Have you ever had a problem that you are certain has plagued someone else and has probably been solved already? It can be frustrating to work away at your particular problem spending time – and possibly money – when you believe the answer to it has been found before. This is one of the reasons that newsgroups were created on USENET when the Internet began; after all who needs to re-invent the wheel?

Here is an example; not too far-fetched, I hope.

Bill has a pond full of fish in his garden. The trouble is that, because the pond is so dirty, he is not sure how many fish he has. He has tried several bottles of chemicals, taking advice from his friendly pet shop. His pet shop may be very helpful, but he cannot rid himself of the thought that it has a personal stake in selling him these different products. A friend directs him to a couple of newsgroups that might help – rec.ponds and rec.aquaria.freshwater.goldfish. (An explanation of the group names will follow soon.)

He figures that the goldfish group may be interesting, but there is nothing wrong with his fish, just his pond water. Asking the ponds group for help, he soon gets several replies from people who seem to have had his problem and have found a solution to it. He narrows down the replies to one that praises a micro-filter pump that looks as if it might be useful. Coming back to the group again he asks more questions about the pump and receives several replies, one of which refers to a mail order catalogue. He asks the person who mentioned the catalogue and finds out where to obtain it. He gets the catalogue, likes the specification and price of the pump, orders it and installs it. This may or may not be the answer to his problem, but he is a lot further down the road to solving it than he was when asking a self-interested salesman for help.

There is a hierarchy to newsgroups, which needs to be understood before discussing groups and certainly before looking for groups that might be of interest to you personally. In order to classify groups as meaningfully as possible a system similar to that of the classification of organisms is used. The broadest classification is on the left of a group name and is followed by sub and sub-sub classifications. In biology a chimpanzee is known by order, family, genus, species – i.e. Primate (order), Pongidae (family), *Pan troglodytes* (genus, species). The classification is narrowed down more the further right one goes. In newsgroups the classifications are separated by periods, so comp.ai.games means a newsgroup devoted to computer discussion about artificial intelligence in general, but more specifically about its application to games.

There are several major categories for newsgroups:

comp Computer sciences and topics related to computers.

news Groups concerned with the news network. This contains groups that will be of great assistance when first starting, for example: news.announce.newusers and news.newusers.questions.

rec Recreational activities, arts and hobbies.

sci Scientific research groups.

soc Social issues.

talk Self-explanatory and long-winded.

misc Just about anything that does not fit easily into the previous groups.

Another collection of newsgroups comes under the heading of Alternative Newsgroups. The major grouping here is the alt hierarchy. Here is where you will find some off-the-wall groups, their titles defying all previous hierarchical descriptions – alt.barney.dinosaur.die.die.die being just one typical example. There are groups devoted to passing pictures back and forth taking up a significant proportion of the network traffic and bearing names beginning alt.binary. Within this alt hierarchy anarchy may reign, but it is where a writer will find some excellent groups to join. Judging by the frequency with which certain names appear in some newsgroups there appear to be writers who live their lives within these groups. (Hey folks! Get out more!)

Some groups begin with a country code; uk.comp.os.linux for instance is a British group (uk) that discusses the computer (comp) operating system (os) linux. You should be able to work out what us.arts.tv.soaps discusses. The group starting 'de' is for Germany and starting 'fr' for France, and so on. Discussions in these groups are usually in the language of that country, but there will often be somebody who will talk to you in English if you find a group irresistible.

It is possible that your Internet Service Provider (ISP) – the company that connects you to the Internet – has its own newsgroups devoted to discussions of problems with ISP-specific software, services provided, announcements and more. These newsgroups are not necessarily available to people who do not subscribe to that ISP and will probably begin with the name of the ISP; e.g. Demon (a large UK ISP) has groups such as demon.announce and demon.ip.support.mac. If you are new to the Internet or you are having problems with ISP-specific software, it is advisable to look into these groups for a while. Problems you may have or questions you may wish to ask concerning general Internet use can be quite easily addressed here and the people you talk to will often be using the same software. Using these groups you will probably avoid the 'If you used MicroSerf's Deplonk you would not have this problem' type of advice: namely, advice that is not really advice at all.

The ISP that you use will govern the newsgroups to which you can subscribe. Some ISPs will allow access to all newsgroups; some may restrict access, usually rejecting the sex-oriented groups. If you wish to have unrestricted access then that will be part of your criteria for selecting an ISP. That selection process is dealt with in Appendix 1.

How to find *your* newsgroups

On your very first access to your ISP the part of your software called the newsreader should automatically connect to the news server and download a list of all the newsgroups that your ISP makes available. This can take quite a while on the initial contact, but on subsequent connections the list will only be updated with changes, which should take just a few seconds. Once you have the list, you may begin the selection process.

It is not possible to describe in detail how your particular newsreader will present the available groups as all software differs somewhat. There are some programs that only deal with mail and newsgroups, either as stand-alone programs or as part of a suite, and there are those that have these facilities built into the program along with a Web browser and other capabilities. In general, there should be a way for you to browse the long list of groups that has been downloaded and also a way to search the list for topics of interest.

Using the ISP Demon, which takes 33,059 newsgroups (at my last count), just as an example we can see the following search for groups of possible interest to writers. Searching for 'writing' yields:

alt.fan.dean-stark.writing	alt.startrek.writing
alt.writing	misc.writing
misc.writing.screenplays	rec.music.makers.songwriting
sdnet.writing	sff.writing
ucb.extension.class.telewriting	umn.local-lists.writingc
wpi.techwriting	zetnet.interests.writing
alt.writing.scams	sff.writing.craft
sff.writing.sfreading-protocols	sff.writing.language-abuses
sff.writing.eugene	sff.writing.business
sff.writing.eternity-ltd	sff.writing.writers-block
sff.writing.utah-writers	sff.writing.dreamweavers
sff.writing.novel-dare	sff.writing.interactive

sff.writing.how-we-read	sff.writing.marketing-strategies
sff.writing.response-times	sff.writing.dreaming

Searching for 'writers' yields:

alt.html.writers	alt.union.natl-writers
christnet.writers	fur.stories.writers
mail.screenwriters	ncf.sigs.writers
torfree.writers	york.fes.writers-cafe
alt.christnet.songwriters	sff.romance.writers
sff.horror.writers	sff.workshop.writers-groups
sff.fantasy.writers	sff.science-fiction.writers

It is probably best to start your search on a broad basis and narrow it down to specifics if necessary. Therefore, out of all these groups the two it would be reasonable to check out first are alt.writing and misc.writing, as they appear to be of the broadest interest. In fact, they are very broad indeed. It would be my guess that every writer who has ever subscribed to newsgroups for writing will have visited one or both of these at some stage.

These are both very busy newsgroups, usually having a hundred or more messages (known as posts) a day. You need to subscribe – this is free – to get their flavour; it cannot be encapsulated in a few words.

If you have very specific needs, as Bill with his dirty pond had in our example, then a search for 'ponds' or 'goldfish' or any keyword relevant to your need will soon yield a few newsgroups that you can sample for usefulness.

From the list of groups above it can be seen how specialized some newsgroups are. The names in the list are mostly self-explanatory. You can take a stab at guessing ones that are not: *torfree* is a Toronto-based newsgroup, for instance. Subscribing to the others would soon tell you what the newsgroup was about. Unsubscribing from these groups is easily done, so you lose nothing from trying out as many as you like. Do remember that traffic may be quite light in any one newsgroup, so do not abandon too quickly a group that seems to have no messages; give it a week or so before you unsubscribe.

If a newsgroup has 'moderated' after it in the listing it means that at least one person 'owns' the group and is a kind of group mom. That person – who was normally elected by all interested parties when the newsgroup was formed – will read the messages sent to the group before they are made available to readers. Off-topic discussions, rude behaviour and anything else that is not considered worthy of the group will not reach the outside world, being filtered first through the moderator. Most groups are unmoderated and thus free of any censorship.

Newsgroups are free and it should not take more than a week or so of subscribing to a newsgroup for you to see if it would be worth your time continuing to subscribe, especially as most have low traffic levels. Extremely busy groups such as alt.writing are the exception rather than the rule.

Another great way of finding newsgroups that might be of interest to you is to use My Deja – more on this in the section on the World Wide Web in this chapter (see page 23).

Threads and how they work

Most newsreader programs, if not all, will automatically organize the posts that are downloaded from the Internet, firstly into the newsgroups to which they belong and secondly into sub-groups or threads within that newsgroup.

Consider a series of posts to a gardening newsgroup.

The first post consists of a question; for example, 'Here are the details of my garden soil. Can anyone recommend a flower type to grow in it?' The questioner has written 'Flower Types' in the subject line. This is now called the *subject header*.

Several people reply to this post suggesting different types of flower. The newsreader will group these together, usually in date order, so that they can be read in conjunction with each other. These following posts will have subject headers 'Re: Flower Types'. The headers are not necessarily visible to you, but your newsreader program will be aware of them.

Someone now comments on one of the replies, saying that the type of flower recommended has not grown well in their garden. This starts a thread within a thread as others comment on this minor departure from the original question. Extra comments may lead to new branches until the thread becomes a tangle. All the posts will usually have the same subject header and will stay grouped together, but it can be hard to figure out exactly where the thread runs unless your newsreader has a graphical layout of posts.

In Figure 1.1 a thread from alt.writing is shown as displayed by the Turnpike newsreader. Expired posts are denoted by a

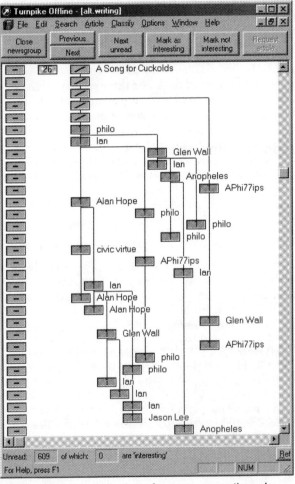

Figure 1.1 A graphical display of a newsgroup thread

backslash in a box and 26 active posts are shown with their respective relationships displayed graphically.

With such a display it is possible to select sub-threads within the main thread and follow them if you wish. Without it you will have to follow the thread sequentially, usually in order of time of posting, and work out who is referring to what yourself. You are helped by the fact that when replying to a post the news software usually quotes the text of the post you are replying to within the body of your new post. You can cut some of this text to shorten your message if you wish. Anyone else reading your concise and erudite reply can see what text you are replying to as well as your own words.

Fortunately newsreaders have the ability to time-expire posts and can be set to keep news for anything between one day and forever. My own preference is for three days in a busy group, a week or more in a quiet one. In any thread only the older posts will be expired, leaving the newer ones. This keeps down the amount stored on your hard disk and keeps the threads down to manageable levels. Even a three-day turnover period can mean a group such as misc.writing having 300–400 posts on it at any one time and as many as 60–70 in one thread.

If you are interested in preserving the posts in your own archive you can set the keep time to forever and then use the archiving facility that your news software should have to remove older messages from display, thus keeping everything manageable, while keeping them stored in another folder on your hard disk.

Joining newsgroups

Once you have subscribed to a newsgroup then you are recommended to read the posts to it for at least a week or two before you contribute to it. This will give you the chance to get to know the major contributors, the general flavour of the group and what is and is not generally accepted as permissible types of message, comment, question, etc.

Many people who subscribe to a newsgroup do not contribute, but only read the posts. They are known as *lurkers*. Someone who has been reading posts for a while and who then begins to contribute is said to have *de-lurked*.

You can pick up a great deal of information by lurking; there is no law that demands your active participation in the group, nobody who sees you watching and demands that you pull your weight by saying something. It is possible that all the questions you want to ask will be asked by somebody else and that you will get the answers to those by following the threads after the posts that pose the questions. It *is* possible, but it is more probable that a large number of the questions that *you* want answered will not be asked. Joining the group actively enables you to ask those questions. It also enables feedback on comments you make, which can be useful and sometimes infuriating.

There are many questions asked that have been put to the group countless times before. This is where the 'FAQ' comes in. FAQ stands for Frequently Asked Questions and many groups, especially the moderated ones, have a FAQ list posted every so often – maybe once a week or once a month – so that the newsgroup is not continually swamped by the same questions being asked again and again – and, of course, answered again and again. It also decreases the boredom level of having to read the same posts repeatedly. There are only so many times that you want to read a question such as 'Which end of the pencil do I write with?' after all, never mind reading the answer again or even answering it yourself. (If you think that is a gross exaggeration then stand by to be surprised. You will be amazed at some of the questions asked online.)

If you ask a question already dealt with on the newsgroup FAQ, you will be branded a *newbie* or just pigeonholed as an idiot. Because good nature and the ability to use a computer and modem do not necessarily go hand in hand, there are quite a lot of Net users who see no difference between a newbie and an idiot.

If you are new to the Internet it will be pretty near to impossible for you to pretend not to be a newbie and get away with it, but you can easily persuade the majority of newsgroup subscribers that you are not an idiot by obeying a few simple rules.

* Read the FAQ list (if one is available).

* Do not jump into an ongoing thread with comments if you have not followed it from the start – unless you want to pick up on a comment or two that is blatantly incorrect.

* Be polite. Remember that smiley faces (or emoticons) – look at this symbol sideways :-) – were invented for a purpose.

The hastily written word can sometimes be misinterpreted and ending a sentence that is meant to be funny or ironic with :-) can help avoid misunderstanding. See the glossary for a small selection of smiley faces.

♦ Do not become irate at some smart answer to a question you have asked that seeks to put you down. There is usually someone in the group who will be sympathetic and will try their best to help you. Smart put-downs often come from people who would not be much help to you anyway. There is also always the possibility that you have fallen victim to the above problem and have misinterpreted the meaning of the response.

♦ Remember that when you hit the reply button on your news-reader or mailing software it will usually copy the text to which you are replying into your own message. This is great for replying to short messages, but take care that you do not send 500 words of original message back to the newsgroup with your 'I do so agree,' text tacked on. Doing this just increases the volume of traffic on the group with-out adding anything worthwhile and will drive many people mad. It also marks you as stupid, lazy or a newbie, or a combination of all three.

Surviving being 'flamed'

In the real world when a group of people with similar interests gather together one of the first things that they usually do is talk to each other, engaging in general conversations – for example, a ticket queue for a pop concert. Larger gatherings can lead to polarization of interests into groups, whose 'cliquey' conversations barely interact with other groups – at a cocktail party perhaps. Still larger gatherings of polarized groups may occasionally interact in an aggressive way that in turn can lead to violence – say a large cocktail party at the end of the evening. As with much else, in the case of newsgroups the Internet reflects life in the real world.

There is little doubt that large newsgroups collect their fair share of egos. Long-term contributors can come to feel that they own the newsgroup in some way and that in an unmoderated newsgroup they have somehow earned the right to moderate the discussion. These self-appointed champions may imagine a slight in an innocuous post or may take exception to a viewpoint held by a contributor. Being able to have a tantrum at a safe distance, they frequently feel unrestrained by normal codes of civilized behaviour and will fire off a post to the newsgroup in terms and language that they would never dream of using in a face-to-face confrontation. This is known as a *flame*.

An angry response from either the unlucky subject of the flame or from someone else leaping in to flame the flamer may lead to what is known as a *flame war*. If you are sitting outside the flame and watching, it can all be very entertaining; indeed some people post what is known as *flamebait* – posts that are deliberately written to start a flame purely for their entertainment. That aside, if you are the subject of the flame it could be upsetting – how much depends on your sensitivity.

If you are upset, then my advice is to ignore it all. If you wish to respond then be rational and reasonable in your response. Whatever view of you the flamer has formed is not going to be changed by any reply from you. Sadly there are people out there who can offer very sound advice with one post, question the parentage, intelligence and sexual proclivities of some hapless poster with the next post and then send generous, helpful comments with another. Others never seem to do anything but flame. Fortunately the majority are well behaved. You will soon learn whom to ignore, whom to read with interest and whom to read with care. And unless you get a real kick out of it all, my advice is not to start or contribute to any flames. Life is too short.

Some people will deliberately post incorrect information hoping for lots of replies from others wanting to jump in and correct the post. They enjoy seeing who cannot resist showing their knowledge to be greater than the originator of the error. These posters are sometimes called *trolls* – as are their posts.

1.2 The World Wide Web

Imagine you are reading a book about mystery writers. Halfway down a page you find the name of one you have never read. Interested in what she might have written you press her name on the page with a pencil and, within a few seconds, the page changes to a list of her published works. One looks interesting and pointing again with your pencil to a book title changes the page to a review of the book. The review says that '…her description of a difficult necropsy is…' You press a square at the top of the page and it changes to a dictionary where you can refresh your memory as to the meaning of necropsy. Another press takes you back to the review.

Finishing the review you think that you like the sound of the book and decide to buy it. A few presses of your pencil later and your favourite bookseller, with whom you have an account, has your order and will be sending you the book – at a price below normal retail – by return of post.

One press of your pencil later and you are back to reading your mystery writer's book again.

The book that lets you do all this is the biggest book in the world – the World Wide Web. The page is from a Website and is on your computer screen; the imaginary pencil with which you point is a mouse cursor. The pencil press is a mouse click on a special picture or line of text. Each page of the book has links to other pages and other books or Websites. The program that displays the Web on your screen, known as a Web browser, holds Ariadne's thread to guide you back along your path as you click from one page to another, because you will get lost in the labyrinth without it; with it your starting point is never more than a couple of clicks away.

The Web is now the centre of the Internet for the majority of users. Companies are falling over each other to have a Web presence; academic institutions are making more of their resources available on the Web all the time. It cannot be repeated often enough: the Web is growing larger by the minute. Hundreds of new Websites are appearing each day. And what exactly, you may ask, is a *Website*?

A Website is no more than a collection of files sitting on a remote computer and sheltering under the umbrella of one address. Your browser asks to be connected to that computer by using an address system. These addresses look strange at first sight, but can be easily understood when you know how they are constructed. Let us take the bookselling company Amazon as an example – after all, it is where the books you write may end up being sold. Amazon has six addresses at the moment, but is expanding its interests so may have more as you read this – remember the Web is continually growing and changing. The first address is **http://www.amazon.com**, and a second is **http://www.amazon.co.uk**.

The construction of Web addresses is, perversely, the opposite of newsgroups in that the address broadens in category from left to right, rather than right to left. The final name in the hierarchy tells you which country the site belongs to; 'uk' for Great Britain, 'de' for Germany, etc. When there is no country ending it is assumed to be based in the USA. The next name, right to left, tells you what kind of organization runs the site and is called the *top domain*.

Some top domains:

ac	Academic institution (UK).
co	Company (often UK).
com	Commercial enterprise.
edu	Educational (USA).
gov	Government body.
mil	Military (USA).
net	Network resource provider.
org	Research or charitable organization.

ICANN, the 'official' Internet naming authority, is introducing several new top domains, including **biz** and **info**. Several companies are now entering into competition with ICANN, hoping to provide even more new domains to cope with the massive increase in Internet use, so you may soon run across some more new names aimed at specialized users.

Some country codes:

au	Australia	**ca**	Canada
de	Germany	**es**	Spain
fi	Finland	**fr**	France
ie	Republic of Ireland	**il**	Israel
it	Italy	**jp**	Japan
nl	Netherlands	**no**	Norway
nz	New Zealand	**se**	Sweden
uk	United Kingdom	**za**	South Africa

As you move further left along the address, so the category narrows until you reach either the furthest left or the name just before www.

Here is the breakdown of two Amazon bookshop addresses:

www.amazon.com: A commercial company called Amazon that may or may not be American and is on the World Wide Web. The computer on which the site is held is probably in the USA.

www.amazon.co.uk: A commercial company called Amazon, on the World Wide Web and held on a computer in the UK.

The whole address is called a *URL* (Uniform Resource Locator) and is really the name of a remote computer connected to the Internet. When you call a domain name with your Web browser either you or your browser need to tell the remote computer what file you want to download. A forward slash (/) after the domain name tells the computer you are now looking for a file or folder on that computer. Just as your own machine stores files in nested folders or directories so that they can be organized and found easily, so does the domain. The first file looked for in the root folder of the domain computer is usually called index.html or home.html. This is called a *default page* and calling up www.amazon.com will normally automatically load that page for you, once again depending on how your browser works. With Internet Explorer, for example, **www.amazon.com**, **www.amazon.com/** and **www.amazon.com/index.html** will all find the default page.

If you knew that a file called '**glossary.html**' was stored on a computer with the domain name **www.ty.writers.com** and held in a folder called '**editing**', you could get to it directly by setting your browser to **www.ty.writers.com/editing/glossary.html**. Connect to the Internet and your browser will take you directly to that page and display it.

A well thought-out Website will have links – highlighted text or special pictures – on the default page which will enable you to navigate around the site easily; you will not need to know where the files are kept, just click on the appropriate links and you will get to the ones you want. A badly constructed site can be a nightmare to navigate.

URLs begin with a name that tells your browser what sort of protocol (or language) is being used by the machine you reach. It can tell you what kind of site to look out for. A URL beginning **http://** will connect you to a 'standard' Website carrying the sorts of pages we have discussed. One beginning **gopher://** will be a site that contains lists of files available – an older system than the Web and very much more restricted in usefulness. A protocol that enables you to select a file from a list and directly download it begins with **ftp://** and one that starts with **news://** will access newsgroups. Your browser will almost invariably be configured to try http first if you do not include it in a typed-in address, i.e. if you type **www.dummy.com** it will assume that you mean **http://www.dummy.com** and try that server first. By the same convention a Web address in this book is assumed to begin with **http://** unless otherwise stated.

Search engines

As you may imagine, to find your way around the Web you will need some assistance. The task of an ordinary librarian with a catalogue pales into insignificance when the volume of data on the Web is compared to a normal library. This is definitely a job for Conan the Librarian.

Fortunately for the sake of sanity, various means for discovering Websites relating to specific topics have been developed and, even better, most of them are free to use – for the time being. These Web catalogues are generally known as *search engines*.

Some of the major search engines are: Excite, Yahoo!, MSN, Lycos, and AltaVista. Fuller details of the comparative strengths of the different engines will be found in Chapter 3. This section gives an idea of what these engines do, how they do it and how to use them.

The Microsoft and Netscape browsers have dedicated search buttons on the toolbar. Clicking these buttons gets you to a page on the default search engine offered by the browser or one you have selected as the default yourself. The engines all have their own addresses and can be reached individually, for instance Yahoo! at **www.yahoo.com**.

Once a search engine has been reached a box will be displayed for text entry. Alongside this will be a button labelled 'Search'. Enter your search text and click the 'Search' button and the engine will go to work. Each has a slightly different approach to how it deals with the text input.

Many engines now have slightly more intelligent searches than they once offered. It is well worth pressing the button on the Web page labelled 'Hints' or 'Tips' alongside the box where you enter your search word(s). This will tell you much more about the engine's specific requirements for phrasing searches. Even if you are an experienced user it is worth checking the tips out once in a while as the way in which engines organize their searches changes every now and then.

A more detailed treatment of searches will be found in Chapter 3.

The Web and newsgroups

There is a Website called My Deja, found at **http:// groups.google.com**, which is an excellent site for finding newsgroups that suit you. The default page is well laid out and self-explanatory. You can search for past messages of interest using keywords and see both the relevant messages and the newsgroups in which they were posted. You may find a message useful to you in a newsgroup that sounded unpromising and be led to subscribe to it. Equally you may find that the newsgroup you thought would be great for you never seems to have discussed your interest and might not be worth your time after all.

My Deja is also useful if you happen upon a thread in a newsgroup new to you that has been going on for a long while. Because of the way that posts are expired by the USENET servers you may not see the first parts of the thread. If you are interested you can read those posts in My Deja.

1.3 E-mail lists

E-mail should require little explanation, even to someone never connected to the Internet. I doubt that anyone, except perhaps those living in the depths of the Amazon basin, will not have a basic idea of what it is. There are extensions to it, however, that you may not have come across and e-mail lists are one such extension. Lists are similar to newsgroups; indeed at least one program that I know of, and probably more, can deal with lists as if they were newsgroups, filing them and expiring them in exactly the same way. An e-mail list is set up on one computer (a *server*) and is often run by a single individual acting as administrator or list mom. *Robots* (programs that run without human intervention) run many lists with an administrator overseeing the messages; some are purely robot run. The server will probably be running more than one list, some of similar interest, others very different.

Messages are sent out by you as e-mail to an address on that server (in the form listname@domain-name) and are re-sent from the server as normal e-mail to all the subscribers to the list. Some servers offer you the choice of either sending you the mail as they receive it or sending you a digest every so often – once a day or perhaps more frequently depending on volume of traffic.

E-mail lists are set up for people who want to discuss a single topic of interest. The topic could be as narrow as wedding dress design or as broad as writing. Lists are usually more intimate than newsgroups in that the number of subscribers tends to be lower and messages stay more or less on topic – most of the time. Out of all the subscribers there are a small number who form a core of regular contributors while the majority lurk and the atmosphere is a great deal more friendly than in a newsgroup – very little flaming goes on because an individual can be barred from the list if they overstep the mark.

Finding lists that suit you

If you subscribe to a writers' newsgroup then you already have one good way of finding a writing list – the newsgroup itself. You can be sure that many people in the newsgroup will subscribe to lists – they may even run one themselves. Members of a list often become like an extended family, sharing hopes, ideas, fears and emotions, and are usually fiercely proud of their list and its other members. Contributors whom you may never meet can become close friends and will interchange personal messages off-list as well as joining in with correspondence on-list. Because of this you will sometimes see information regarding lists included in a signature (three or four lines at the end of an e-mail with author's name, internet address and other – sometimes amusing – messages), especially if the writer is running that list. If you see an address, subscribe and try it, it will cost nothing and it is as easy to unsubscribe as to subscribe if you find the members and/or the subject material are not to your liking.

If you cannot find any list addresses in the posts to the newsgroup you could ask the group in a posted message. 'Does anyone know of a good mailing list for writers?' would be fine. You will have many replies to pick and choose from. My advice when you ask is that you are not too specific about your subject needs. Many groups have topics which vary wildly from day to day and you might deter someone from recommending their list if they feel that it does not fully fit your demand. Take what is offered, try it and if you do not like it, try another.

One good Website to try is **http://www.groups.yahoo.com**; another is **www.liszt.com**. Between them they have several thousand lists, sorted by category, and you should find something to suit you. A good site in the UK that has a catalogue of mailing lists is **www.author.co.uk/ezine**.

Search engines can be used to find mailing lists too. Results are variable. One search engine on the Web gave a response of 25,900 sites when queried for 'mailing lists'. This was reduced to 3053 when the search was for 'mailing lists writing'. These searches can yield some anomalous results; the last mentioned search reported the City of Berlin Symphony Orchestra Website as part of its return.

Subscribing and unsubscribing

If a person runs your list, then you will be able to start or end a subscription by mailing them with a normal message in plain English. You will also be able to mail this human administrator directly with any questions you may have to ask. There will normally be several addresses connected with the list. As a fictitious example take a mailing list called mylist that is run by a company called mailinglist. To subscribe or unsubscribe you might send mail to **mylist-subscribe@mailinglist.com**. To ask any questions about the list the address **mylist-administrator @mailinglist.com** may be used. To receive help on FAQs or to learn how to switch your mail receipt off for a short period when away on holiday a robot may send a help file when you mail **mylist-help@mailinglist.com** – actual instructions may be sent as a message 'set mylist nomail' to **mylist-**

request@mailinglist.com. Finally, actual posts to the mailing list that the group will all read will be sent to **mylist@mailinglist.com.** Any mailing list that you join will have slightly different address formats for these and you can get them from your list administrator when you join.

If a robot runs the list, then there will be an exact format you need to follow and a special address for sending the mail to. Usually the subject of the e-mail will need to be what you want to do, i.e. subscribe or unsubscribe; sometimes the body of the e-mail needs to be the action followed by the listname. Either way the format should be spelled out on the server for the list.

Many lists can be subscribed to from a Website. This will normally involve e-mail but may sometimes mean filling in a form presented on site. Full instructions will be given on the Website as to how to go about subscribing and unsubscribing.

If you want to annoy the other subscribers to the list when you no longer want to belong you could just keep mailing plaintive and useless 'Unsubscribe me' messages to the list address to be read by the whole group until someone has had enough and tells you exactly what to do. (See previous newbie/idiot references.) It is better to keep the instructions you will be given when you join so that you can deal with it yourself.

Receiving the list as a digest

There is a major problem with subscribing to a list and receiving it piecemeal: with an active list you will be flooded with e-mails that can be hard for you to administer. If your program can treat that e-mail as a newsgroup and file it accordingly that will help, but the flood of mails remains the same. A digest, sent at regular intervals dependent on the amount of traffic in the list, will contain everything that has been sent to the list since the last digest; it is *not* an abridgement or précis. Receiving the digest can be compared to receiving a newsletter from a group of people you have come to know and trust, and who share similar interests with you.

One downside of a digest is that it will not be organized into threads, leaving you to sort out what posts are referring to; another is that it can be out of date. If somebody asks a question or, in a writing group, sets a fun task such as 'Write a story explaining the meaning (not necessarily the right meaning) of the following word:' then you may miss out, getting the digest long after the moment for replying has gone and probably after most of the others on the list have replied. Digests may give a certain feeling of remoteness and spoil the immediacy of a list. If your fellow contributors are in a time zone hours removed from yours there may be little immediacy in the group anyway, the main traffic taking place during your sleep period and flooding your mailbox when you connect to the Internet in the morning at the time when other members are asleep.

If your list server offers a digest then you can probably switch from immediate mail delivery to digest and back again easily, so why not try both methods and see which one works best for you?

Starting your own list

You have searched the Internet for a mailing list that suits you and have failed to find it – what next? Why not start your own?

The companies that run mailing lists – Yahoo! groups (see page 28) is one – will usually enable you to start a list without too much fuss. There is a difference, however, between just starting a list and starting a successful list. The first thing you need is contributors. You will need to advertise it, maybe on your own Website, maybe in newsgroups. If you choose the newsgroup route you will need to be careful. Advertising in newsgroups, even self-advertising, is frowned on by many Net users and, even if you think you are trumpeting a good cause for a sound reason, general announcements to all and sundry about your fabulous new list will, almost certainly, earn you a flame or ten. Be subtle. Why not put the address in your signature along with a pithy message? Or you could directly e-mail people in the newsgroup you have come to like and trust, and ask them to join the list. That way you would start with a group of known contributors that others might eventually wish to join.

Starting a list is not for the faint-hearted. It will not be an instant success; indeed it may never succeed at all. Even if it does succeed, once up and running it will be out of your control – it may run away in a direction you never imagined, to concentrate on topics that bore you stiff. You may even wind up watching it die on its feet after a successful run. Administering the list will take up your time. However, people who run lists have told me that they have a lot of fun doing it, so try it if you want to – what have you got to lose? It will not cost you money.

By the way, if you need to be told in this book how to start your own list, you are not ready to start one. There is help out there in the form of mailing lists, and Websites that run lists will be of assistance to you, but if you cannot find these yourself you are, again, not ready. You do need a reasonable amount of Net experience before you take this step.

1.4 Web communities

You will come across the word 'community' in many places on the Web. A community in the Internet sense is very similar to a newsgroup or mailing list. People with like interests will connect to a Website, select their community page and read the messages posted there. They can also post their own messages to the community. The site will provide other services such as links to resources and other sites of interest.

There is often a *chat room* available that you can 'enter' with a simple mouse click so that you can 'talk' (via the keyboard, naturally) to other members who are connected at the same time as you. This is similar to IRC, discussed in a moment, but anyone who is part of your community is probably going to be more productive to talk to than someone found by chance on an IRC channel.

One major difference between communities and the mailing lists described already is that with Web communities the posts are retained by the server. Looking at two Websites that host communities, Yahoo! groups (**http://groups.yahoo.com** – see Figure 1.2) and Topica (**www.topica.com**), the home page for each mailing lists has a box in which you may select one of several options, as well as subscribing to the list. In order to be able to process these options you will need to join the service. This is free and involves entering your e-mail address and a password and waiting for a confirmation reply by e-mail. You can set your browser to remember the password for future log-ons. The service will now keep a record of the groups to which you are subscribed and give you full access to them.

Once logged-on and at the home page of the list, you may set your preference to 'individual mail' (Yahoo! groups) or 'messages'

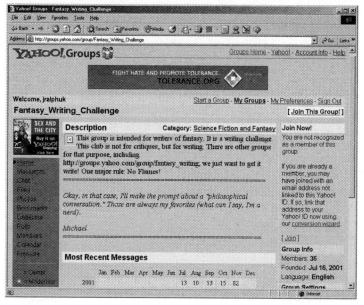

Figure 1.2 A typical home page for a community at Yahoo! groups

(Topica), which means that all the posts to the group will be sent by e-mail to you. You may choose 'digest'. Or you may choose 'Web only'. In the last case nothing will be sent to you and all transactions (reading and posting) take place while online; the ability to browse and compose posts at your leisure while offline is not available. This might not be a problem if you are not paying any online or phone charges, but if you are you can rack up some serious bills in the course of being part of a community. If you choose to receive mail or a digest you might never visit the Website; all you need to do can be accomplished with your normal mailing software.

There is something awfully compelling about the Web; more people are choosing it as their sole means of Internet use and moving away from the older type of interface. The colourful graphics and the easy, one-click links have a fascination with which simple text transfer and offline-reading cannot compete. However, I cannot see communities taking off in the UK until phone charges are drastically reduced.

A number of these communities can also be found on the site **http://communities.msn.com/**. Plenty of other sites are available, some sites for a single community, some, like the MSN site, for multiple communities. Access to the MSN site is free; other sites such as the Well (**http://www.well.com**), one of the first free community sites, now charge a monthly fee for membership.

The MSN site has a facility on the home page that searches on keywords, where a search for writing returned 2026 communities on the MSN site alone. A general Web search will lead to many more. In short, writing-related Web communities abound and are easier to find via the Web than by the older methods described above.

All comments in this book regarding newsgroups and mailing lists should be taken to include the Web communities. The community is really just a new way to present them, so advice about one is advice about the other.

1.5 IRC

IRC stands for Internet Relay Chat. Numbers of server computers are linked into networks such as the Undernet, EFnet, and DALnet. These networks provide areas for discussions that are known as *channels*. Special IRC software will connect you to a network where you may view the currently active channels and join them for multi-way conversations. It can be compared to CB radio except that response time is a lot slower, and I do mean a lot. Anyone can start a channel and name it. Once open, anyone can join and converse. IRCers give names to channels reflecting the topic of conversation that they wish to have. The names run from boring, through mundane to obscene.

My personal view is that I have better things to do than indulge in boring, time-lagged, typed conversations with mostly adolescent males (probably spotty), with nicknames like Iceman, Obi-Wan, Stallion, Paladin or Tharg, whose interests are rarely above waist level when they are not talking about computers or *Star Wars*. It is also true that a large proportion of users with female-sounding names are similar, spotty boys. Using a female name – whether or not you really are female – can also leave you open to adolescent pestering. That said, there are unquestionably lots of folks who can happily lose themselves for hours on a chat channel, just as CB radio has its passionate advocates. I repeat, it is my personal view – as you may have guessed from the tone of this paragraph.

One possible good use for IRC is as a long-distance telephone. If you arrange with a friend to set up a channel at a particular time, you can enjoy a very cheap conversation, albeit with long periods between responses. The chance of someone joining your conversation uninvited is quite high. Even though software will tell you when someone does listen in, you cannot afford to be too confidential in what you say.

Connecting to IRC

A special program, extra to your browser but one that works with it, known as a plug-in or a completely independent program – mIRC for instance from **www.mirc.com** – is needed to connect to IRC server computers and get you chatting.

IRC servers have names like: **datashopper.dal.net** (DALnet Denmark), **us.undernet.org** (Undernet USA) or **eu.undernet.org** (Undernet Europe). A list of sites to connect to should come with the program.

Details for running the software and a full explanation of the command language used – sometimes known as the 'slash' commands – will also come with the program you choose to run. If you get hooked on IRC, stand by for huge phone bills and hours of unproductive fun.

1.6 ICQ

Pronounced as 'I seek you', this software enables something approximating a permanent IRC connection. Download the ICQ program from **http://web.icq.com/** and install it. During installation the software will ask you to register at one of a broad network of servers. At this time you will be allocated a Universal Internet Number (*UIN*) that is unique.

In future, whenever you log on to the Internet the software will announce your presence to the servers, and anyone who has the ICQ software installed on their computer and your UIN in their selected list (and who is also connected to the

Internet at the same time) will be told that you are logged on. Equally if you have their UIN in your list, you will be informed that they are online. A simple click on an icon and you can be communicating with them directly, chatting, sending messages, exchanging files and more.

Using this program can give you a slight advantage over IRC if you want to 'converse' with a friend or colleague. Setting up a time when you will both be on the Internet is all you need to do. No arranging of a specific channel is necessary. When you are both logged on at the agreed time your software will tell you and you can just 'talk'.

Another gain over IRC is that you only chat to friends and contacts whose number you know; there are no random visitors. A disadvantage here is that you will not meet new people this way, although you can seek out people with similar interests to you. See the program for details.

1.7 File Transfer Protocol (FTP)

Small files can be easily transferred from one computer to another by using e-mail. When dealing with large files, such as programs or a big data file, a much more efficient means of transfer can be used: this is FTP or File Transfer Protocol. An FTP site contains files – often thousands of them. There are two ways to use FTP: directly from your browser or with a separate, dedicated FTP program.

Connecting to FTP servers

Here is an example of using a browser to download a file using imaginary addresses.

During your intrepid surfing you have come across a site offering shareware programs and you rather like the look of one that will generate characters' names for your latest novel. Along with a short description of the program might be a button reading 'Download this program' or a piece of appropriate text might be highlighted. Clicking on the button or text will connect you to an address like ftp://super-shareware.com/misc/chars.zip. After perhaps a question or two, such as 'Do you want to run this file or save it to disk?' and 'Where do you want to save this file?', your browser will begin to download the file, saving it to the disk folder you have specified and showing you a small graphic telling you how it is progressing in the download. You should still be able to use your browser while the file downloads in the background. When the downloading has finished the file then resides on your hard disk and can be used at your convenience.

If you know a file you want is at a specific FTP address, you can enter the address manually into your browser and get the file. You will either need to know exactly which folder the file is kept in on the server, or use the default page presented to you, to search for the file. Once you have found it you can download it.

A dedicated FTP program will allow you to connect directly to any FTP site. Many ISPs have their own FTP site carrying programs and text files of relevance to your ISP's software as well as many other files – **ftp.demon.co.uk** for one. You will be asked to log on with your name and password. Most sites will accept you with 'anonymous' as your name and your Internet address (yourname@your.domain) as the password. Anonymous FTP will allow access only to certain areas of the server's file system – typically a folder called 'pub' and its sub-folders.

Use the program to get to the folder and file you want in order to download it. Graphical programs such as WS_FTP are good (see Appendix 1 for a site to obtain it).

There will be more on FTP sites and file finding in Chapter 4.

1.8 ISP forums

There are several ISPs that offer more than Internet connection. These services offer access to their own private areas, areas not accessible to non-members, and because of this they are sometimes known as *added content providers*. They also charge relatively heavily for their services and a comparative discussion of the merits of standard ISPs and these providers will be found in Chapter 7. CompuServe and AOL are two major ISPs of this type and they provide forums for discussions, chat facilities, file access, messaging, mail and other services as well as being gateways to the Internet at large.

Summary

- Newsgroups are great places to get information even if you only lurk.

- With over 30,000 newsgroups available you should find at least one that fits your interests.

- Read a newsgroup's FAQs (if available) and read the group posts for at least a week or two before contributing. You will save yourself some embarrassment.

- Resist joining in flames and try to smile if you are flamed.

- Remember Google's My Deja is always available for past newsgroup posts.

- Join a mailing list or two, either directly or via a Web community.

Exercises

With all the exercises remember the Website that goes along with this book (**http://www.valley.demon.co.uk/**). You will find it a good 'jumping-off' point.

1 Find a newsgroup that covers one or more of your interests and subscribe to it.

2 Think of a large company and try to guess its website by building up an address from first principles. See if you can connect with the site on the web. Try companies in other countries.

3 Find an e-mail list or web community that fits your interest and subscribe to it. If it doesn't interest you as much as you thought it would, keep trying others until you do find one of interest.

By now you should have a good idea of what the Internet is and know enough about its workings to be unfazed by the technical side of the coming chapters. It must be time to learn about some of the things on the Internet that you, as a writer, can enjoy.

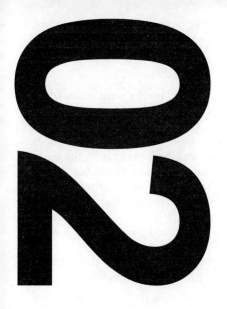

02

writing techniques

In this chapter you will learn

- how to get help with your writing
- about sources for 'how-to' articles

The Internet is a great source of help for improving your writing techniques. As well as articles to read and courses to follow, you can also find and join discussions and crit sessions in newsgroups and mailing lists.

The stores are full of 'how-to-write' books with names like *Writing Fantasy Fiction*, *Fiction Writer's Workshop*, *The Craft of Writing Articles* and so on. They sell well and give good advice. I am quite old-fashioned about books; I love the feel of paper and enjoy the versatility a paperback has – read it in the bath, on an aircraft, by a pool in summer. The one problem with books is that, no matter whether or not you have read a 'crit' before you buy, it is not until you have bought it and read through it that you really know if it is any good to you. It could be money wasted. If books could be provided free of charge it would not matter so much if you read one that was not quite as good as you thought it would be. Out there on the Internet are just those things – free 'how-to' books.

Before you become over-excited, they *are* free, but they are not quite books; that would be too good to be true. What they are could better be described as pamphlets or articles of varying length on 'how-to' rather than 80,000 word treatises. Despite this, there are articles available that contain lots of valuable information and tips written by talented authors, which would easily sell for cash if printed and bound. Why then are they made freely available? Probably in most cases because of the ethos of free information that still abounds on the Internet. And perhaps because the authors genuinely want to help beginning writers. Whatever the reasons, do not dismiss these articles just because they are free.

There are articles on writing in general and on 'genre' writing in particular. Presumably because of the historical background of the Internet and the interests of the majority of original users, there tends to be a concentration on science fiction writing, but definitely not to the exclusion of all else. Screenwriting has many articles, as does mystery writing. General tips on writing, from novels to short stories, can be found. In short, whatever your chosen 'genre' you can be fairly sure of finding some advice about writing it somewhere out there.

One problem that all writers I know suffer from occasionally is the dreaded writer's block. As you might expect, there are many articles giving advice on how to beat this. Advice varies from the sensible to the wacky. I suspect that some of the articles were produced by writers in the throes of block as a way of getting through it themselves. Many of the sites devoted to helping you with your writing have these articles.

There are numerous sites devoted to editing, copy-editing and proofreading. Whilst not directly concerned with the creative writing process these are professions that have profound effects on a writer's finished product. Looking at articles that aim to help those who work on this side of the business cannot hurt a writer. Points of grammar and punctuation should be of interest to any writer and knowing what a copy-editor does as well as the meaning of copy-editing and proofreading marks will help you when proofs of your own work come back from the printer.

One request that is often made in newsgroups is for a recommendation of a writing program. It is unclear whether the person requesting this information is looking for something to help with writing or to do the writing for them. Needless to say there is no magic program out there that will do all the work for you. There are programs that purport to help you with plot lines, some that will generate characters and names for you and some that will help you keep track of characters in a long novel. I cannot recommend them one way or another, but most appear little more than card filing systems with a few 'bells and whistles', or random number generators that shuffle characters' names, occupations and so on like one of those children's books that flip pictures of different body sections to make funny looking composites. If you have a computer to connect to the Internet you will surely have a word processor program that you use. I would suggest that such a program would be what you use for your creative writing. And, of course, the stuff inside your head (sometimes known as wetware) that can never be replaced by anything you will find on the Internet.

However, one program that can be of immense help to a writer, especially one who writes articles or short stories for magazines and thus has a large output of manuscripts, is *manuscript-tracking software*. This will keep a record of all your work, usually with details of dates and word counts and other stuff you might think important, and also track to whom you have sent it and when, what the reply was, and who the MS is with now. It will give you reminders when a set time has elapsed without reply after sending a query out, so that you may send a gentle reminder to the publisher or send a fresh query out to another, and generally helps you remember what stage has been reached in the long process of selling a piece of work.

All these things are very hard to keep tabs on if you are a busy writer, but are nonetheless essential if you are to be in control of the sale of your work. There are several programs available for this task, but one that I have found useful is part of the CD sold with the electronic version of *Writer's Market* (Writer's Digest Books) published annually in the US. It links in with the markets in the CD database and has the facility to add your own markets to an extra database, making it useful for writers in other parts of the world. You can order *Writer's Market* from **http://writersdigest.com/marketbooks/marketshome.html**.

One that you can download if you are living outside the USA (and find it difficult or too expensive to get *Writer's Digest*) that I have also found useful is SAMM. It works with DOS or Windows (so Mac aficionados will be disappointed) and does a competent job of tracking your work, organizing contacts at the publishers you have dealt with and even keeping a tally of how much money an article has earned you. I use it and like it, although one complaint I have is that it will only accept US-format telephone numbers. It is available free from **http://www.sandbaggers.8m.com/**.

2.1 Newsgroups

What newsgroups can do for you

At the risk of stating the obvious, the people who contribute to writers' newsgroups are usually writers. They are certainly not all wildly successful writers, nor are they all excellent writers, but among them are contributors who are, in a quiet way, both pretty good and moderately successful. If you are seeking advice about writing, a newsgroup is a good place to start. There are some reservations, however, that will be pointed out as we go along.

You do not always have to ask any questions yourself in order to learn. There is always someone asking the group about some point of grammar, for a way of changing points of view (POV) in a story, how to best use tenses, do I use quote marks for thoughts, how do I write a précis for publishers, how do I get agent representation and a hundred other topics. Reading the responses to these queries can often give you answers to questions you had not thought to ask but wished you had, as well as questions that you had been thinking about for a while. However, there are times when you find that you just have to ask your own specific question.

A lot of posts in a group can seem hardly worth your time; almost like listening in to a conversation at a party that the people who are talking find interesting, but which you find desperately boring. There are, however, nuggets of gold in newsgroups. There are also times when the silliest of threads will spark an idea in your mind for a piece of work. Do not be too quick to dismiss a discussion as off the topic of writing and ignore it. Most of us cannot afford to miss out on a good idea. Joining in a long humorous thread on toilet paper in one group led me to write an article on my grandfather's life in the coal-mines. These connections do happen in the strangest way.

You can often find these nuggets if you follow a thread that interests you, and questions on writing techniques will lead to them if anything will. Even if you end up finding advice you have read before, it can be useful at times to be reminded of something you had, perhaps, forgotten.

How can you know if the advice is sensible and worthwhile following? If you ask a question about a technique or style, for instance, the answers can generally be categorized as follows:

(a) *No answer.* The ones who could have answered missed your post, were otherwise too busy to respond, or could not be bothered. It is unlikely that your question was considered ridiculous or too easy; had that been the case someone would have been unable to resist the next answer.

(b) *A 'wiseguy' answer.* This comes from people who believe themselves to be too clever for the rest of the world. It is fairly easy to recognize this answer for what it is – as much a waste of space as the originator. Indeed the poster could probably not deliver the next answer.

(c) *A serious answer.* This can be tricky to sort out. Is it worth-while following the advice or not? Is it correct? Could it be totally misleading? If you are a long-term reader of the group and you know the contributor from previous posts, then you can weigh the value of the answer according to your assessment of him/her. You can relate the answer to other things you have read and work out if it makes sense or not. Your best chance of knowing it to be good is when more than one group member responds with the same, or similar advice. There is a pretty fair chance of it being good advice if that happens. And often with good advice comes an answer like below.

(c) *A referral to an article on a Website.* This is the best answer of all if someone fairly well known or well respected has written the article. The referral can have extra value if the Website has other articles of interest to you, or has links to further sites – frequently the case.

The kind of response you get to a question asked on a newsgroup is also dependent on your previous contributions to the group. If you have posted an occasional, reasoned comment or given advice in a knowledgeable way once or twice, then you stand a better chance of receiving a good response than if you have just spent a month or two jumping in with both feet at every opportunity in order to display your brilliance. If you are that kind of person then you will probably not be willing to ask for advice anyway. Frequenters of newsgroups seem to form opinions – sometimes good, more often bad – of other group members rather more readily than in the real world, probably because of the way it is so easy to misinterpret the written word. This misinterpretation is especially true for the hastily written word – post in haste, be flamed at leisure. If the group knows you as a reasonable, polite individual then you will get some good advice when you ask for it.

2.2 The World Wide Web

Finding 'how-to' articles

Once you know a site or two that delivers what you want you are up and running. The kind of site that offers advice on writing will always have links to other, similar sites – unless they are selling a service such as a writing course, and even then they may show some links. Following these links, which have been found by others, saves you a great deal of time and effort in searching – once again, why re-invent the wheel? But how to find those sites in the first place?

Newsgroups are, again, a good place to start. The signatures of regular contributors often have addresses of Websites. These sites in turn have links, sometimes to the kind of site we are looking for: a site delivering information and good writing advice. Following link after link, meandering your way through the Web and bookmarking sites of interest in your browser program, can be rewarding. You will come across sites that you never would have found otherwise and which you find useful. You will, of course, pass through sites of no interest whatsoever as you meander, but that is why the activity is called *browsing*. If you browse in a shop you expect to pick up and put down many items before you find one that you like; it is no different when you browse the Web. Chapter 3 will give you a better idea of how to approach a search engine in the most appropriate way. Until then, here are a few ideas and examples.

A simple search on Microsoft Network's (MSN's) engine for 'articles writing' on the entire Web yielded 195,696 results. The same search on UK Websites yielded only 6319. These results include duplications because of the way the engine indexes sites, but it is still a large number to sift through. Changing the search to 'articles writing fiction' reduced the results to 798 for UK sites, still a large number but much more manageable.

An example of what can be found in these selected sites is the Jacqui Bennett Writers' Bureau site – **www.jbwb.ndirect.co.uk**. Run as a commercial concern and advertising the owner's writing courses, the site still contains useful information for free: a list of UK markets for short stories with helpful guidelines – and there aren't many of those around in the UK – and many links to other sites containing 'how-to' advice.

The USA has the greatest number of sites with this sort of help. Running through the search results gives many routes to sites with advice for free. One site that will certainly be of interest is **www.angelfire.com/va/storyguide/**. This site boasts 1001 links to articles about fiction writing, and it is possible to collect a huge amount of information from the links that the site provides. Another site is found at **www.olg.com/pfwriter** and is a collection of chapters from what might turn out to be a book on fiction writing techniques. Presented by Peter E. Abresch, it is well worth a look. The US site **www.writersdigest.com** has a wealth of information on its site and is well worth browsing. You will find more sites listed in the Appendices.

You will come across many sites that offer courses for fees. While it is up to you whether or not you are prepared to pay for courses – some of which seem excellent in their content and quite good value for money – there are a lot of free and helpful articles available. It might be worth your while to hunt for these first and assess them before you shell out hard-earned cash. You can check out some of these courses by again asking around in newsgroups and mailing lists. You are likely to find someone who knows someone who has used a particular course, or has read comments about it, even if you cannot find a correspondent who has taken the course personally.

If your writing interests do not lie in fiction there are other helpful sites to be found. The previously mentioned 1001-links site has a strong bias towards screenwriting and there are templates for various word processors that can be used for writing scripts in a Hollywood-acceptable layout. There are articles on technical writing and on magazine article writing. Sites for journalism abound. Just plug your queries into the search engine of your choice and sift through the results, remembering that the more specific the query, the less sifting you will need to do.

2.3 E-mail lists

Asking for advice

If you are subscribing to a list that is any good at all – if not then why are you still subscribing? – there will be writers on that list who know more than you do about something in just the same way that you are bound to know more about another topic than they do. Knowledge is valuable and the sharing of it gives most writers a real kick.

For instance, you may have a specific question that you need answered:

> I have a character in my latest story that needs to change his opinion of another in a believable way. How can I best do this without a 'Road to Damascus' kind of conversion?

At least one person on your list may have read a 'how-to' on this topic that you have not. They may have had this exact problem personally and found a way to deal with it. They may know of a Website containing a specific article that could help you. They may be able to point you to a novel where you can read for yourself how another author has approached the problem. Whatever the source of their knowledge they will be glad to share it with you.

You may get this advice from a regular contributor or from a lurker who will de-lurk just for you. However it comes, advice *will* come your way from the list members. The small nature of a list, when compared to a newsgroup, means that the number of people you communicate with is fewer, but the intimacy of a list can make communication easier and better. And the advice is free; you can take it or leave it. Whatever you do, it pays to be polite and grateful; after all, you may want to ask for advice in future. Being able to *give* advice at times leaves you with a good feeling too.

Long-term membership of a list gives you the chance to really get to know the members – at least those that contribute frequently. With this knowledge you may find that a particular problem you have brings to mind a specific member of the list. You can e-mail them directly, rather than throw the problem open to the whole list. Bear in mind that this can be problematic. If you do not like the advice you are given you will probably hurt your respondent's feelings if you subsequently post the same problem to the list; it is almost like a slap in their face. If you want to stay in their good books then perhaps you could ask them if they mind you posting to the list. Maybe you could post to the list thanking your respondent publicly and asking if anyone else has different ideas. Whatever you do, think about how a post of yours will affect other list members if you want to stay welcome yourself.

Some lists will welcome a posting of a short story or part of a novel if you desire criticism. Standards and styles of criticism will vary, but you will be exposing your work to readers outside your own home circle of friends and therefore you are likely to get more objective comments. Exposure of work to large newsgroups can cause an unfavourable reaction, especially if the piece is rather long – remember flames? – whereas the members of a list are much more likely to accept an occasional longer piece for criticism, maybe in the order of 3000 words or so.

If you just throw a story open to your list you must expect all sorts of advice, but you may, if you wish, ask only for editorial advice, for comments on plot lines, for ideas of possible markets that may not have occurred to you or other specific help you might feel that you require. Like most things a list works both ways, so you must be prepared to help with other writers' work when they post it if you expect any advice on your own. Reading the work of others and giving constructive criticism is a valuable way for you to learn too.

Some further advice is that you do not send the same work repeatedly to the list. Resend it once perhaps, but you cannot follow everyone's advice and will either get the same criticism again or no criticism at all from those whose advice you have ignored. Keep resending it and very soon nobody will even read it. They might even be reluctant to read any further new posts you might send.

There are groups that exist solely for the purpose of criticizing each other's work. When you join such a group it is normally a requirement that you help a number of others with their writing problems if you expect help with your own. A typical requirement would be to criticize four pieces to every piece that you submit. Lurking is not normally allowed and if you do not participate over a given period, say a month, you will be removed from the list. You can usually send a message to the listserver to tell them that you are busy or on holiday for a long period. This is referred to as 'nomail' and your particular listserver will tell you how to do it. 'Nomail' will keep you on the list without your needing to participate, but you will not receive any mail. This also stops you from having to sift through hundreds (or even thousands!) of list messages on return from a long holiday.

Finally you may feel that a list has started to get too 'chatty' for you, become too quiet, or you might even feel that you have in some way 'outgrown' it. Here are some replies extracted from a thread started by someone who thought that one particular list (anonymized) was dying and not worth belonging to any more. I hope they give some insight into why lists sometimes seem to change and into why writers enjoy them and find them worthwhile. I certainly obtain a great deal out of belonging (to this list in particular) and from getting to know some really fine people.

Glee: We need each other. …During a golden time on the left bank, many authors emerged from the coffee houses and brothels and salons and wrote more brilliantly than any single gathering of individuals since Shakespeare and Bacon and Marlowe drank in the pubs of London. It was no happenstance, it was a gathering of the minds and they fed one another's intellect. We could be such a resource if we only knew it. We know one another. We have an interest in each other's success. Your success is mine, and mine is yours because we helped each other through this.

Anne: I'll bet the old writers' groups, too, had their times of chat and chaff. Likewise there are ups and downs on *** as well. … I have critiqued a few things in the past few weeks, and I think that's one of the valuable reasons for ***'s existence. I'm not unsubscribing anytime soon…

Jean: I like the freedom on ***… I think the worse thing on a list is to feel that you MUST read it or contribute, as that to me kills the list: unless of course it is that kind of list in intention.

I have always got crits when I specifically asked. However, I want honest straightforward crits even if they hurt.

Gary: I really believe that many novice and bashful writers are helped by lists such as this one. Critiques are free and can be a learning tool for the novice as well as the intermediate writer. Perhaps it's an individual thing. In my own case, I am getting more out of crits off these lists than ever before. They are helping me. I will continue to use them.

Tim: Writing flows through my veins, and much of this conviction comes from the time I have spent on ***. When I first joined I was posting lots regularly, and felt as if I had 'come home' to a large extent. YES, *** IS chatty, but this has REALLY helped me to formulate and develop my arguments and reasoning when debating subjects and even just to hone my skills at relating events in my life. I will be eternally grateful for this. The 'like minds' here have been welcoming to me as a person of a kindred spirit, but we have not always agreed on things. The chance to debate topics intellectually with those in the same camp as well as the 'opposition' (WITHOUT getting flamed) is a rarity on the 'net, and one to be cherished.

If I can't crit because I'm busy, I'm busy, and I have no new pieces to submit for crit either, through lack of writing. A few posts I did put up received no comment at all, and my out-of-joint nose was quickly fixed when I said, "hey, if I'm too busy to read every post and comment, then so is everybody else." It's just a fact of life, and my advice to those posting regularly is to carry on, and not think that we are ignoring you or have lost interest. It comes and goes.

MaryJane: I think at certain stages, list activity (AND participation) is the juice we all need to recharge us, encourage us, and inspire us. At other times you just need a place to kvetch with your peers and friends. *** provides it all, for me anyway. But, yes, I do believe there are times when certain stages of our creativity and productivity need ALONE time, time to eliminate distractions and put our noses to the grindstone, so to speak.

2.4 Newsletters

Newsletters were not covered in Chapter 1 because they are so similar to e-mail lists. You subscribe and unsubscribe in a similar way and at intervals receive, yes, a newsletter. Unlike e-mail lists you do not contribute posts in the same way; it is not a fully interactive process, but more like having a paper newsletter drop through your letterbox every so often.

Newsletters are advertised in – here we go again – newsgroups and on Websites. Finding them in newsgroups just requires reading posts, but finding Websites requires a search.

A simple search on Yahoo! for 'newsletter' provides some 70 categories with thousands of sites, the majority of which have nothing to do with writing. Using Yahoo!'s advanced search facility with an input of 'newsletter AND writing' gives over 50 results, pointing you to several newsletters of interest, some of which are not free of charge. Many of the newsletters that do charge offer a free sample, either of the newsletter itself or of extracts from past issues. Check them out and then it is up to you to decide if you want to pay; meanwhile here are some free newsletters you may enjoy. I am a long-term subscriber to all of them. The descriptions following are of one, typical edition of the newsletters and are shown as an example of their usual contents.

Writing for DOLLARS!: Bi-weekly newsletter. Editor: Dan Case.

* An Australian freelance writes about achieving greater success by mixing photography with articles.

* Magazine guidelines, divided into high, medium and low paying markets.

* A review of a writer's 'how-to' book.

* Classifieds.

* Claimed circulation over 7000. Website: **www.awoc.com**

* To subscribe: e-mail **wfd-request@MailingList.net** with the message 'subscribe'.

Inscriptions: Weekly newsletter. Editor: Bev Walton-Porter.

* An article on repetitive strain injury for computer users.

* A writer-oriented interview with a successful novelist.

* Publishing news and changes.

* New mailing lists of interest.

* A humour section, job opportunities gleaned from elsewhere on the Web, market guidelines, competition news, numerous advertisements and classifieds, book reviews.

* Circulation unknown. Website:
  www.inscriptionsmagazine.com

* To subscribe: visit the Website.

Page One: Bi-weekly newsletter. Editor John Weaver.

* Novel Beginnings: Each edition begins with the first paragraph from one or two books that subscribers are reading at the moment. Great for seeing how published writers draw in the reader with the first words of a book.

* In the Spotlight: Each edition has an interview with a published author that gives a potted biography and some insights into how they succeeded in selling their work. This edition's interview was with Kent Haruf, author of, among others, *Plainsong*, a nominee for 1999 Book of the Year.

- In the News: Publishing news of various kinds.

- The Write Way: A 'how-to' on writing. Published writers give tips on many different aspects of writing. This edition was about getting original ideas. The newsletter gives an address that leads you to a fuller article on their Website.

- Websites of Interest: All writing oriented.

- No claimed circulation figure. Website **www.pageonelit.com**

- To subscribe: visit the Website.

Write to Publish: Monthly (approx.) newsletter. Editors: Trevor Lockwood and Karen Scott.

- This is more of an update on what has changed on the editor's Website – **www.author.co.uk** – than a magazine like the US newsletters above. However, several of the topics covered in each issue referring you to the site have interest and relevance to authors in the UK. The Website is claimed to have 20,000 visitors per week and is well worth a visit.

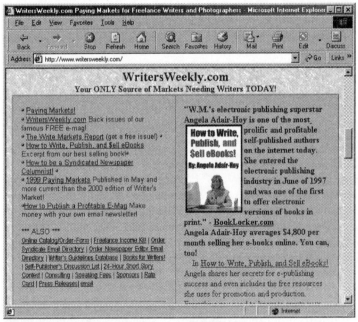

Figure 2.1 Another example of a good 'how-to' and marketing letter, reached at http://www.writersweekly.com

The newsletter is a good way of tracking changes on the site without the need to spend ages revisiting it, which is why it is included here.

* E-mail <**author.co.uk_subscribe@listbot.com**> to subscribe or better still, visit the site first and subscribe from there.

If you get the impression that these are mostly US oriented, then you are correct. However, the articles giving advice on how to write, how to sell, how to cope with rejection, how to deal with writer's block and so on are mostly universal in their application, even to non-English-speaking readers. The publishing business, the creative writing process and the readers of books and articles are pretty much the same the world over as long as you bear in mind the differences in grammar, punctuation and spelling – even in the same language.

It costs nothing to subscribe to most of these newsletters and there are lots out there waiting for you to subscribe. It would be surprising if you could not find at least one or two that held your interest and there are 'how-to' articles in each issue of the above that may give you some new ideas to improve your writing. A long list of newsletters is given in the Appendices to get you started.

2.5 ISP forums

The forums on writing found on Compuserve, AOL etc. are great places to ask for advice. They are so similar to newsgroups that all the comments made under that heading apply here.

Summary

- Newsgroups can help you to improve your writing by offering advice on any queries you might have. Read the group carefully and others may be asking your questions for you. You must assess the answers to queries for reliability.

- Search the Web for articles and courses on writing and ask around for comments on the quality of courses.

- Follow links on writing help pages you find for further help and advice.

- Use the contributors on your mailing lists for advice and pointers to Websites that can help.

- Try to get involved in 'crits' on your mailing lists. You can learn both from 'critting' others' work and from submitting your own to the process.

- Don't give up too easily on a mailing list. They can change in nature from time to time depending on what the major contributors are up to, but they can still be useful.

- Subscribe to newsletters. There are many that are full of good articles that will help your writing.

Exercises

1   Try one of the sites mentioned for articles on a writing genre that interests you. (If you have no luck read Chapter 3 and then try again using a search engine.)

2   Get involved in a newsgroup and/or Web community you subscribed to in the Chapter 1 exercises and see what advice you can get for any writing problems you might have.

03

web search engines

In this chapter you will learn
- what search engines are
- how to use them

The Web is the area of the Internet where you are most likely to do your main research and search engines are what you are most likely to use. They therefore get a chapter of their own. It is worthwhile emphasizing once again that the Web is not a magic resource. It is not a replacement for conventional research, merely a supplement to it. However, it is a very good supplement and repays the effort expended in learning to use it.

In Chapter 1, I mentioned that search engines are a database of site addresses held in the form of catalogues. I also invoked Conan the Librarian. He is the engine and the database of addresses is his library card file. Give him a subject to look for and he will flex his muscles and search for the sites you need in his catalogues.

The catalogues, or indexes, are automatically compiled by computer programs (called robots, crawlers or spiders) that search the Web for new sites and collect their addresses, or are compiled by real live humans from manual searches for new sites or from addresses submitted by site owners. Some are hybrids, where robot-gathered information is sorted and supplemented by human intervention. The gathered addresses are linked to keywords that describe, or are taken from, text on the site, so that when you enter a word into the search engine it can display all sites that are keyed to that word. For the purposes of this book the term *search engine* will be used to describe the automatic listing engines, the human-compiled directories and the hybrid versions. Different engines have different databases, site collection programs, search requirements and site ranking schemes.

Where once the search button on your browser would always lead to a selection of engines from which you could choose, the newer versions of browsers tend to offer just a default engine. For instance, Internet Explorer now gives you the MSN search engine by default. While this is good you might want to try another and so will need to keep the addresses of engines that you like bookmarked in your browser. This way you can call them up with a couple of mouse clicks whenever you like. Of course you can delve into the browser program and change the default to your favourite engine, making it only one mouse click away. (See your browser Help file for the way to do this.)

3.1 Logical or Boolean operators

Most search engines let you use logical operators to restrict searches; these operators use *Boolean logic*, which is a big name for a simple idea. The operators vary slightly from engine to engine and familiarity with their use is highly recommended. Major logical operators used in Boolean searches are AND, OR, NOT, brackets and/or quote marks. The best way to demonstrate this concept is to use an example.

Imagine that your aim is to find sites giving some information about crime fiction books. You could start with a one-word enquiry: crime. This would lead to so many sites with no relevance to your interest that it would be a complete waste of your time. Just imagine the thousands of sites that will cover law enforcement!

Your next move might be to increase the number of search words giving a sequence such as: crime AND fiction, thus asking the engine to return only pages that have *both* crime and fiction in their text. This would yield a much better result as a search, but you may miss out on some sites that could be of relevance to you since many crime novels are described as mysteries.

A further refinement might be: (crime OR mystery) AND fiction. Crime and mystery are inside brackets because you want the search engine to work on those two words together – to look for pages containing both the words crime and fiction, and also both the words mystery and fiction. Now you are more likely to get results that you want. Without the brackets the engine may search for crime OR (mystery AND fiction) giving pages with just crime again as well as pages with mystery and fiction – almost equivalent to the first one-word search. Leaving mystery out on its own, by swopping the order of the first two search terms, will lead to pages that discuss the pyramids or the *Marie Celeste*.

If you do not want anything that refers to Agatha Christie or Martha Grimes – I cannot think of a reason why, but merely use it as an example – you might decide on a query like: (crime OR mystery) AND fiction NOT ('Agatha Christie' OR 'Martha Grimes'). Placing the names within quotes tells the engine to treat them as phrases and placing them between brackets tells the engine to work on them together.

Further refinements are possible as all the operators can be used in any combination. If your search were to be too general with the above example, perhaps crime AND mystery AND fiction might tighten up the parameters. Getting the search as tight as possible and then widening it if necessary is often better than the other way round. It is very hard to deal with hundreds of results, even harder with thousands.

Almost all the engines will accept what is known as 'search engine math'. The plus sign '+' is used at the start of a word and is the direct equivalent of AND. The minus sign '–' is used at the start of a word and is the direct equivalent of NOT. Phrases or strings of words placed within quote marks are assumed to have '+' before them and the search engine will not only look for those words in a document but it will also look for those words in the order in which they are given. Thus the last but one example above would read: crime mystery +fiction –'Agatha Christie' –'Martha Grimes'.

Search engines that use Boolean logic will give a brief account in their search tips section of how they may use operators in a slightly different way from other engines. Here is a summary of the logical operators at the main search engines.

♦ **AND**: Finds only documents containing all of the specified words or phrases.

   Support: All except for Google, Infoseek, LookSmart and Yahoo!. All except LookSmart support the use of '+'.

♦ **OR**: Finds documents containing at least one of the specified words or phrases. It is possible that more than one can be found in the same document, but not necessarily.

   Support: All except for Google, Infoseek, LookSmart and Yahoo!. Google will prevent an OR search and the others take OR as a default when met with a string of names.

♦ **NOT**: (Sometimes EXCEPT or AND NOT are used.) Excludes documents containing the specified word or phrase even if the document contains those words found in a search with AND or OR.

   Support: All except for Google, Infoseek, LookSmart and Yahoo!. When using these engines the term AND NOT must be used. The '–' symbol is accepted by all except Google and LookSmart.

- **NEAR:** This specifies how close two words have to be in a document before the engine calls it a match. The exact distance is not changeable by you, but depends on the engine. For example, looking for Turbo NEAR Dodge will reject pages where the two words are too far apart.

  Support: AltaVista – within ten words. Lycos – within 25 words. WebCrawler – within two words.

- **Brackets:** (Sometimes known as nesting.) These will separate terms from the rest of the list so that any operators inside the brackets will be used just on those terms or an operator before the brackets will be used equally on terms within them.

  Support: All except for Google, Infoseek, LookSmart and Yahoo!. The order in which nested phrases are processed may differ from engine to engine.

Some writers can apparently manage to sit before a clean sheet of paper or a blank word processor screen and write a successful book straight off without preparing an outline before starting work. I am certainly not one of those writers and I suspect they are very much in a minority.

Just as it would be foolish to attempt committing pen to paper or fingers to keyboard without a good idea of what you want to say and how you intend to say it, so it would be foolish to approach Internet research in a similar fashion. The key to effective research is preparation. Think your search through before you submit it to an engine. In the long term you will save both time and effort.

If an engine supports Boolean terms or search engine math then see how that engine uses them and learn to use them for anything other than the most straightforward search. Do not be put off by the name Boolean; it describes something that is quite easy to use. Like many things, when you understand it you cannot believe how complicated it can be to describe something so simple.

3.2 Search engines and using them

Documents, archives, encyclopaedias and more are all online and most are easily accessible through your Web browser. The key to successful research on the Web is good use of the search engines to find your material. As mentioned above, a little thought and a few minutes' preparation before beginning a search will save hours of unproductive (if interesting) browsing. To begin with you will need to know a little about search engines.

A detailed description of each engine is hard to give. The engines are subject to the same forces of change as the whole Web and they alter their natures over time, sometimes slightly, more often drastically. The databases of some are used by others and the way they are used changes as time passes. However, it is safe to say that a search on a specific database is usually better done through the engine that owns it.

There are take-overs going on all the time and the flavours of an engine are changed by their association with a new, dominant engine. Frozen in a moment of time, here are descriptions of some of the major engines. The comments contained in the descriptions are a personal opinion. Further and more detailed descriptions can be found on The Search Engine Watch at **www.searchenginewatch.com**, which gives information on the latest progress in the many search engines. The site also gives details of other engines not included in this restricted list.

Although parts of the following descriptions may appear complicated at first, the search engines are designed to be user-friendly – with a varying degree of success. Using them a few times should clarify anything that you might find confusing in these descriptions.

AltaVista

www.altavista.com or **www.altavista.co.uk**

AltaVista has been one of the largest engines on the Web since its inception in December 1995 and has been consistently trying to stay among the leaders since then.

In October 1998 a new selection of search features was made available using its own and other databases. Normal Web searches now give up to four different sources on the results page, more sources hopefully leading to more relevance.

The Ask Jeeves service (see below) is used for its Ask AltaVista service, aiming to give a link to pages that exactly match your request. If you make a search for 'software' the service will

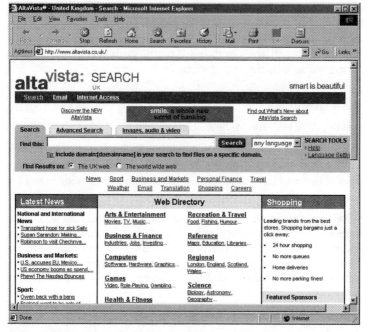

Figure 3.1 AltaVista UK home page

respond with a question like 'Where can I find reviews for software?' Selecting the answer button alongside that question will lead you to a site containing reviews.

LookSmart (see below) is also used for directory listings. The AltaVista version of the directory is used to match categories after Web page displays in a section called 'AltaVista Recommends'. From AltaVista's home page these categories can also be selected and topics listed for browsing.

AltaVista has tried to do away with the need for placing quotes around phrases for which to search. For instance, West Yorkshire as a search should lead to exact matches with the two-word phrase. The company says that millions of phrases have been built into a dictionary and your text entry will be parsed for phrases that will be searched for.

The ranking system whereby the results of a search are presented in an order showing less relevance to your search as you proceed down a long list of sites may be misleading; it is allegedly possible for sites to pay for higher ranking.

The AltaVista service is good, delivering a high number of relevant pages and the use of other search engines as a cross-reference is helpful. There can be large numbers of duplications in the results, and the databases have recently been reported as being some months out of date.

Ask Jeeves

www.askjeeves.com or **www.ask.co.uk**

Fully available for use since June 1997, Ask Jeeves is a search engine powered by humans. It searches its own database at first and, if unsuccessful, it will use other engines to provide matches. It has an original approach to queries.

The engine uses a technique whereby, after giving it search words, you are presented with a list of questions. Clicking these questions leads you to further, refined information. There are claimed to be over 7 million questions compiled by human editors in its database from which a selection will link with your query.

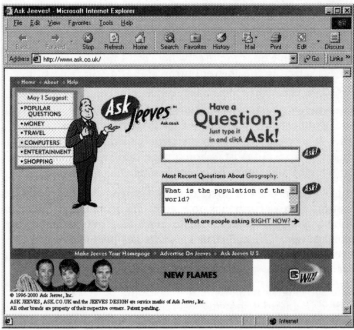

Figure 3.2 Ask Jeeves UK home page

An example of a search is probably the best way to explain Ask Jeeves's different way of searching.

When asked: 'What is the best search engine for research?', Ask Jeeves replied with three questions for further searching.

'What does the computing term search engine mean?'

'Where can I find comparisons and reviews of search engines?'

'What is the best search engine?'

Clicking any of these leads to lists of sites relating to the question.

Jeeves suggested two more questions that might be of interest and 42 matches to Websites from WebCrawler, InfoSeek, Yahoo!, Excite and AltaVista were returned. Most sites appeared to be fairly relevant.

Ask Jeeves will also list the most popular questions that other searchers are asking at the moment – not necessarily of much use to a serious researcher, but perhaps of interest if you are browsing.

Do not be afraid to ask the engine the exact question that you want answered. You may be surprised how often it will return a sensible answer.

Excite

www.excite.com or **www.excite.co.uk**

Launched in 1995, Excite is a popular search service. In 1996 it took over the Magellan and WebCrawler services. It 'powers' the results of Netscape and AOL NetFind's searches.

Searching is aided to a certain extent by suggesting extra words for you to search on based on your initial entry. The words are fairly close matches and can offer avenues to explore that you might otherwise have overlooked. The end result of a search using the Excite engine is not necessarily wonderful. There are usually a large number of irrelevant hits – sometimes as much as 50 per cent of total results – and a fair proportion of duplicates, where one page is referred to several times. The advanced search offers the ability to construct complicated searches using Boolean operators.

In 1999 Excite developed a targeted approach to queries. A quick example is the best way to describe how this works. A search for 'New York' will return a result page headed by a city

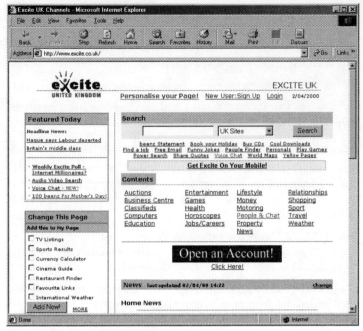

Figure 3.3 Excite UK home page

map, current weather and resources for tourists. Adding a word to make the search 'New York weather' will give current weather and an extended forecast. US universities, geographical names, large companies and some other words and phrases will act as triggers for this targeting.

News-related searches are quite good with Excite, as are those that are music-related.

HotBot

www.hotbot.lycos.com or **www.hotbot.lycos.co.uk**

HotBot is another well-used engine, similar in popularity to AltaVista. Launched in 1996, it relies on two main sources for its information, Direct Hit and Inktomi.

Direct Hit looks at a number of search engines and refines results by looking at what results users click on. Sites with high click-rates get higher rankings, a technique that sometimes works well and at other times is meaningless.

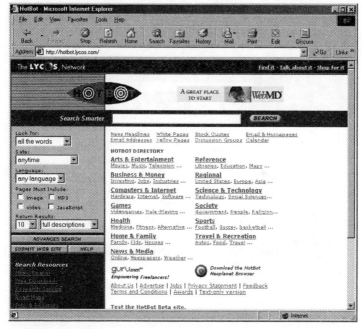

Figure 3.4 HotBot home page

Inktomi was originally a search engine based at Berkeley University in California. It is now used only as a large index to power other engines. The engines using Inktomi personalize the search service they offer with the index by filtering and ranking, so that results from searches on different engines will differ, even though the same index is being used.

HotBot returns fairly high numbers of irrelevant pages and duplicates, but seems to be very good at being up to date, few results leading to dead sites. Its advanced search page is non-Boolean, presenting a number of drop-down lists from which parameters such as date, geographical location and language of page may be selected, along with various word filters that produce the same effect as Boolean entry terms.

Infoseek

infoseek.go.com

Infoseek started in early 1995 and has a smaller index than most engines. With Disney, Infoseek is the producer of Go

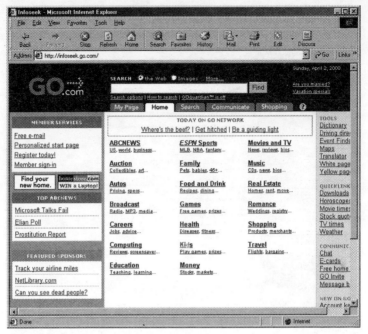

Figure 3.5 Infoseek home page

(**www.go.com**), a portal offering personalization and free e-mail, with Infoseek search facilities.

Infoseek consistently returns highly relevant pages in its results. It is rare for the links presented to not work, implying a frequent updating of its index. An advanced search page offers drop-down lists in similar way to HotBot, but not quite as detailed. Despite the high quality of results, the lack of access to really high-powered searching is a let down.

LookSmart

www.looksmart.com or **www.looksmart.co.uk**

One of the larger directories, LookSmart also uses the AltaVista database if no results are found in its own. It offers a 'Top ten most visited' link to Direct Hit and a service called LookSmart Live, which provides e-mailed responses to queries. Several other engines use the large LookSmart database. It has no advanced search facilities and returns seem to be randomly sorted.

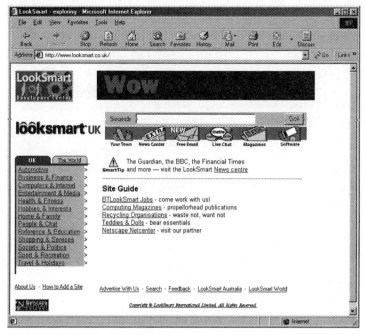

Figure 3.6 LookSmart home page

Lycos

www.lycos.com or **www.lycos.co.uk**

In April 1999 Lycos changed direction from being a robot-harvested engine to a human-compiled directory and in October 2001 relaunched again with an improved service. It has a directory based on the Open Directory project and supplements this with a robot-harvested index. Lycos owns HotBot, a service that is run separately.

Results of a search are laid out so that 'Sponsored Listings' (i.e. sites that pay for display) are separate. Under 'Web Results' you will find sites from crawler-based listings provided by FAST, the engine used by Google, and listings from the Lycos service are noted as 'From The Lycos Network'. Open Directory listings are now accessible through category links at the bottom of the results page, sometimes offering a better chance of narrowing down your search than the offered numbered listing.

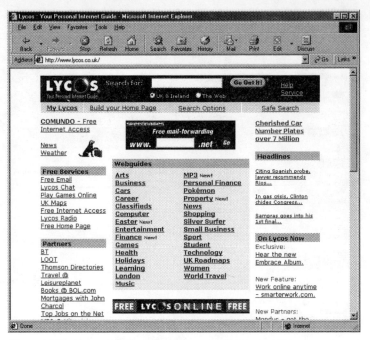

Figure 3.7 Lycos UK home page

The human editors working on the Open Directory number over 10,000. Even assuming that with so many voluntary editors there must be some who are poor, the editing power far exceeds that of Yahoo! (page 67), which has less than 200 editors on its staff. Questions been raised over the possibility that business interests at the Open Directory may lead to inappropriate promotion of sites, but even when this possibility is considered, the expertise and broad variety of specialist knowledge available could lead to a valuable resource in the near future.

MSN Search

www.msn.com or **www.msn.co.uk**

After several manifestations, the MSN service settled down in late 1998 with directory listings and search engine results having Inktomi as the power behind them, although as this is being written a change to using the AltaVista database is, apparently, in the offing. The LookSmart database is also used.

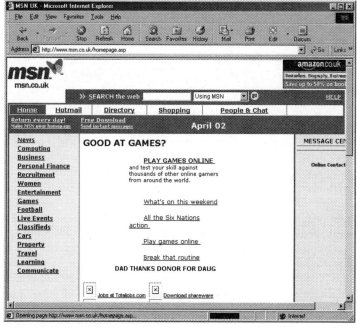

Figure 3.8 MSN UK home page

The MSN search is tightly linked into Internet Explorer (IE). Although other search engines can be set as default in IE, when MSN is selected an 'Autosearch' option is available. Microsoft has in excess of 40,000 popular queries with pre-programmed responses. If your search fits with these popular ones you will find the results are excellent, if not then it does not give much of an advantage. You will be better off using the – very functional – advanced search features of the engine.

Northern Light

www.northernlight.com

With no end in sight to its growth, Northern Light now boasts an index of over 130 million Web pages – in contrast to AltaVista with a reported 150 million and Inktomi with 110 million. Test queries carried out have implied that Northern Light returned more matches than any other engine, a finding that Northern Light declares makes it the largest index on the Web – using some logic-chopping to back the claim. Until there is a standard search benchmark, claims like these need to be regarded with some care.

Northern Light provides a comprehensive search page, with the ability to select date ranges, sources and subjects from lists, and to limit documents to certain categories.

A service that searches for articles published in over 5000 publications is also available. The index is called the Special Collection. Searching is free, but articles are downloadable only after a fee is paid. The Internet writing community has been abuzz with the implications of this service. An author who has written an article for, say, the *LA Times*, has been paid by them for the rights to publish. Allegedly, Northern Light says that they may sell that article over the Net without the need to recompense the author again even if the rights sold were 'one-time' rights. Northern Light says that the publishers they get the articles from tell them that they own the rights. There has been pressure from a number of authors to boycott the Northern Light service for this reason. If the problem of copyright and compensation to authors for the re-sale of their work has been resolved, I am not aware of it at the time of writing.

Northern Light has another URL, **www.nlresearch.com**. This site defaults to searching only the Special Collection. If you have your browser set to receive cookies (see glossary) you will find yourself redirected to this URL even if you want to go to their main search URLs. Set your browser to reject cookies if you want to visit this site and return to the normal Northern Light site later. (See your browser help file for details on how to do this.)

Open Directory

dmoz.org/

A large database owned by Netscape and run by volunteer editors. All the entries, many of them submissions from Website owners, are selected by the editors.

Lycos, Netscape and HotBot are among several engines using this database.

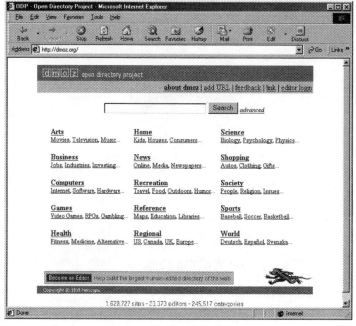

Figure 3.9 Open Directory Project home page

Yahoo!

www.yahoo.com or **www.uk.yahoo.com**

The first choice for many searchers, Yahoo! has been around since 1994 and has a well-deserved reputation for ease of use. With its own database supplemented by that of Inktomi, it delivers matches from the latter after matches from its own.

Yahoo! is a good engine to use if you are certain that you know the category of the subject you are seeking and want many links to it. Because it is a directory service, the index has been handpicked and you can be moderately sure of relevance in returns.

Many of the engines now provide specific search sites for the UK and/or Europe and other individual countries as shown by the co.uk addresses given above. Another such site is UK Plus, found at **http://ukplus.co.uk/dynamic/ukplus/index.html**. These engines move away from the heavily US-oriented major

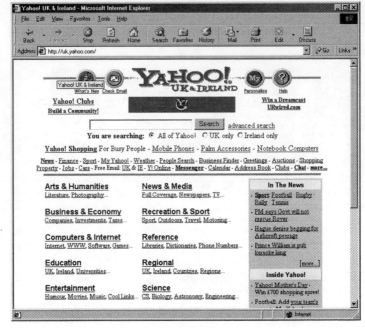

Figure 3.10 Yahoo! UK home page

sites, but their use can be more restrictive; after all the majority of Websites are in the USA, even if they may be rather parochial in outlook when read with non-American eyes. There is always the opportunity to search the whole Web from the UK-specific sites as well as to confine the search to the UK (and Ireland).

The way that engines rank sites, displaying the highest ranked sites for you first, is not completely effective – nor is it totally trustworthy. As mentioned previously, it is not unheard of for sites to pay for higher rankings, thus getting their sites presented before other, perhaps more relevant, sites. The Webcrawlers look for text in the Web pages they find and record it. It is simple to construct a Web page that contains text that is hidden to the normal browser, but readable by the crawler. This can lead to site builders including screeds of irrelevant text that will push their site high in the rankings. There are other techniques for increasing the rank of a Website in a search engine's listing. The bottom line is that rankings should be viewed with a jaundiced eye. Figure out for yourself what use a site might be to you from its address and the short description of the site that the engine shows. And do not give up after seeing just ten sites or so described. Look a bit further into the list of sites returned.

3.3 When one engine is not enough

As well as all these individual engines there are now meta-search programs that sit on top of a number of engines, query them all and sift the results. PC programs include Web Ferret (**www.zdnet.com/ferret/indev.html**) and Copernic 2001 (**www.copernic.com**). Without prejudice, let us take Copernic as a typical example of these programs.

Copernic offers various categories for your search. These include the Web, newsgroups, e-mail addresses, buy books, business and finance, games, health, kids, life, movies, music, newspapers and others. More categories may be added by contacting the Copernic Website.

These categories hold their own selection of search engines. For instance, the Web category might use AltaVista, Euro Seek, Excite, Fast Search, HotBot, Infoseek, Lycos, Magellan, MSN Web Search, Netscape NetCenter, WebCrawler and Yahoo!. Other categories use different engines appropriate to category. These engines can be added to or reduced in number.

The program will automatically update its search engine parameters when connected to the Internet, adding engines or categories and modifying or removing engines as changes take place on the Web, so that after an update the engines it will use to search a given category might well be slightly different from the ones you have seen it use before.

Searches can be of three basic kinds: search for all words, search for any words or search for an exact match of phrase. The first is equivalent to using AND, the second to using OR and the third to using brackets or quote marks. The 'Refine' button on the toolbar can be used to enable full use of logical operators such as AND, OR and NOT on search engines that use them, and to modify a search in other ways.

A type of search can be selected that limits the results for you. Quick search gives ten returns from each engine with a total of

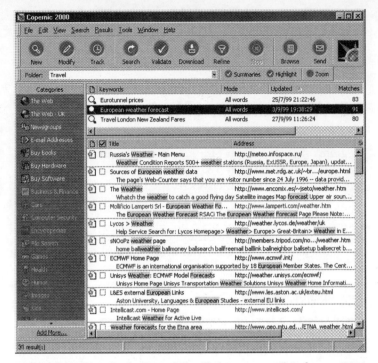

Figure 3.11 Result of a search for European weather forecasts on Copernic

100 results, Normal gives 20/100 and Detailed gives 30/300. A Custom setting will give a maximum of 300 returns per engine with a limit of 1000 total returns. *Results* are pages that the program has found and believes fit your search and *returns* are the pages that you are shown. The more you restrict the number of matches that each engine returns, the more chance there is of a page that would be of interest to you being cast aside because it is further down the list of results than your cut-off point for that engine. However, the larger the search you allow, the more time it will take and the more returns you will have to sift through.

Further, these returns are graded as percentage hits, where '100%' fits your search exactly and then reduces according to fit. The list of returns can be sorted by page title, Web address, score or engine. Search results are kept on your hard disk. They can be easily arranged into folders so that results from different searches can be organized. This means that the results can be examined offline before looking at any sites of interest when you re-connect to the Internet.

The use of programs such as Copernic means that many engines can be searched simultaneously, thus greatly reducing the time needed to find a given topic on the Web. If you have a favourite engine that you know will find a site on the subject you require it may be quicker to use just that single engine. If you are trawling in the dark, then one of these meta-search programs may be exactly what you need.

The Web also has meta-search engines that trawl various other engines. You may already have noticed that Ask Jeeves is a meta-search engine in that it uses several other engines to seek its results. There are many of these meta-search engines now available. In my opinion, one of the best ways to access these is through SearchIQ (Figure 3.12) at **www.zdnet.com/searchiq**, which holds links to many of the meta-search engines. It also grades them according to its own scheme and can offer suggestions on which to use depending on your type of search.

The advantages of using one of these Web engines rather than a computer-based one such as Copernic is that you have a little more flexibility in the meta-engines you choose. You may find one that suits your research line particularly well. The disadvantage is that, unless you save the results yourself, either onto disk or by printing them out, you lose them as soon as you turn off your browser – with Copernic your searches are saved for you in an organized fashion on your hard disk so you can look at them again later or even modify a previous search and try it again.

The search engine Google (**www.google.com**) is worth a separate mention. It relies on a different approach to working out the relative importance of a Website and is at present the only engine to list PDF files, MS Word, Excel and PowerPoint documents, Rich Text Format and PostScript files. IBM is working on the 'Clever Project', which has a similar approach. Instead of looking at just the text on a Web page, the links displayed on the page are examined. Pages on the Web that cover space exploration, to give an example, will have a high probability of referring to the nasa.gov site. The more Websites that link to nasa.gov, the more nasa.gov rises in the relevance stakes as far as space exploration is concerned. An assumption is made that

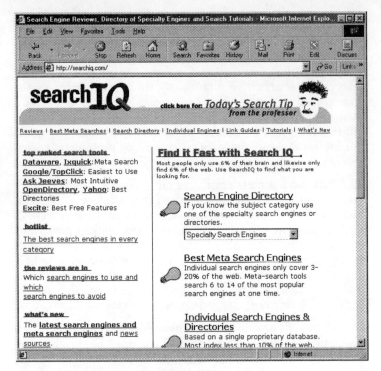

Figure 3.12 SearchIQ home page

the more links to a site that are found throughout the Web, the more authoritative the site. IBM refers to such a site as an *authority* and calls sites that tend to refer to these authorities by giving many links to them, *hubs*. An authority should be a site with excellent information on the topic concerned – space exploration and nasa.gov in our example – and a hub should be only a step away from an authority in reliability because of its readiness to cite the authority. At first glance this argument may seem circular; in practice the results appear to be encouraging. Look out for increasing use of this technique. You will find an interesting feature article on this technology on the *Scientific American* Website – surf over to **http:// www.scientificamerican.com/1999/0699issue/ 0699raghavan.html**.

3.4 General search tips

The best tip of all is to prepare your search. There are really two approaches to searching. I call them the shotgun technique and the laser technique.

With the shotgun you start with a wide search and narrow it down until you – hopefully – find your specific target. This can take a lot of time and can lead you astray in the process as you browse down various promising avenues – not in itself a bad thing sometimes, as browsing can lead you to an unexpected and rewarding find.

With the laser, your search is targeted so precisely that, to begin with, you stand every chance of getting no results at all. Your subsequent searches depend on how you widen your parameters and the results will differ if you do the same search again, widening it in different ways.

There are ways to find sites without using a search engine and when you cannot find what you are looking for with one. It is possible to guess at the URL of a site if it belongs to an organization you think will cover what you want. Start with www and add the name of the organization, or an abbreviation for it, or an acronym that it might use (e.g. ford, amateurastronomy, ibm). (Remember that some characters are not allowed in names, forward slash '/' for instance, and that amateurastronomy could also be amateur_astronomy, where the separator is an underline symbol, or amateur.astronomy or other variations.) Add the appropriate top-level domain name and country if applicable (e.g. .com, .co.uk, .ac.de) as described in Chapter 1, plug the result into your browser and try it. If you are using US spellings then try British spellings and vice versa. If you are unlucky, then think of alternative names until you get it right or you give up. You cannot settle for being almost right in an Internet address, you have to get it exactly right. Internet Explorer now tries to help here, as it will automatically look up on MSN search any address your browser fails to find. It will offer other possibilities for the site if it can. As ever, this is sometimes useful and sometimes not.

A page for which you already have a URL may return 'page not found' – a dead link. If this happens you might get somewhere by cutting back the URL you have from the right-hand end up to the first '/'. Keep cutting and you may reach an index that gives you a route to the page you are seeking or to an equally useful page. For example, you may have a link to a page with an address such as www.dummy.com/writing/science_fiction/eddings/mrin_codex.html. If this is unavailable it might be because the page has been removed; re-addressing as www.dummy.com/writing/science_fiction/eddings/ may give you an index of everything in the eddings folder. If this does not work then try www.dummy.com/writing/science_fiction/ and see what is indexed there. This technique does not always work, but when it does, it saves you the time it might take to track down the page – or something similar – using search engine.

Often you will be automatically re-directed when the page is moved; in this case just bookmark the new location, delete the old bookmark if any and read on. At other times the page may have been completely deleted, in which case you may never find it. If you are really desperate to find it then look at any e-mail addresses in pages near the top of the site, especially on the site's default page (in the example above www.dummy.com). A person running the site may be able to help you, even if it is just to tell you that the page has gone for ever.

Use the ability of the search engines that operate category and subject search restrictions. These may get you to the top levels of sites that you can then mine for information. These search restrictions will narrow down your results and make it easier to find pages that will be of use to you.

Try to find unique keywords or combinations of unique keywords that will cut down on the irrelevant returns from engine databases. Try using the search limits that your search engine offers – search for 'only URL' or 'page title' for instance.

Read the help files at the search engines you use. Print them off your browser and study them to see how you can use the extended search parameters they offer.

Bookmark, bookmark, bookmark! It takes a second to bookmark a site you find interesting; it may take hours to find it again.

When you get to an interesting site do not neglect the links displayed on it. You and the site owner must both have an interest in the same topic so any other sites that they have thought worthwhile to link to are highly likely to be of interest to you and might not be easily found otherwise. If you come across a site that you find really useful and that is part of a Web ring (see glossary) your luck is in. The ring will lead you through many useful sites.

There are sites – and pages within sites – on the Internet that are not and possibly never will be catalogued by any engine. This could be because:

* The site requires a login and/or password for access and robots cannot enter it.

* The site has specific code on its index page that forbids robots to extract information.

* The site is commercial and therefore limited in access.

* The page(s) are on an Intranet, i.e. are part of a private network and are not necessarily linked from anywhere outside that Intranet.

* The page(s) are in a coded format that is inaccessible to robots. Adobe Acrobat PDF files are a good example of this. (See Chapter 6 for more on PDF files.)

The only way you will learn about sites and pages like this are if someone tells you about them and even then you still may need authority to gain access to them.

Two very good sites will keep you up to date with changes in search engines and give detailed comparisons. The first has been mentioned already, **www.searchenginewatch.com**, the second is **www.notess.com**. Search Engine Watch will e-mail you with updates if you so choose. You may also subscribe and have access to more detailed information should you require it.

Summary

- Prepare your search before jumping into a search engine.

- Remember the shotgun and the laser techniques.

- Find a search engine that fits your research and your preferences and use it as the default in your browser.

- Use the meta-search engines for fuller, quicker coverage of the Web.

- Try a meta-search program and see if it suits you.

- Always bookmark a site you find interesting.

- Follow the news on search engines and try the new ones.

- Do not be afraid to ask your writing friends if they know of an engine that might be of use to you for some specific research.

- Do not give up too easily when a search is fruitless. Try other engines. Rephrase your search or change the type of search.

- On sites that look halfway promising follow any links – they might have what you are looking for.

Exercises

1 Think of a search you wish to carry out, sketch it out on paper (using Boolean operators if necessary) and then try it in as many search engines as you can.

2 After the above exercise you should have found a search engine and a keyword-search strategy that seems to work best for your search. Now try a completely different search and see if the same engine still comes out on top.

3 See if you can sort the engines used above into groups (or individual engines) that best fit the different topics you are researching.

4 Use one or more of the meta-search engines for some searches. Check to see which single engines used give the best results and then bookmark them for future use.

04

internet research

In this chapter you will learn

- where to find sources for research
- how to access sources for accuracy
- how CDs can help your writing

You can research just about anything on the Internet. Libraries, university sites, newsgroups, mailing lists, file and shareware archives hold amazing quantities of information – though its quality and accuracy should never be taken for granted!

The Internet is bigger than the biggest library in the world and though it does not have all the books online that, say, the British Library contains, the British Library itself has an Internet site and titles held by it can be checked out for relevance to any research you might have in mind (**http://portico.bl.uk**). The Library of Congress is also available (**http://lcWeb.loc.gov/homepage/lchp.html**).

There are a large number of books held as electronic text on the Internet that are available for downloading. Some are connected with Project Gutenberg (**www.gutenberg.net** – of which more later on in this chapter), some are found in academic and university sites and some in other sites dedicated to a particular subject or author. Not all of these are downloadable for free, but then not all research needs entire books, either. Newspapers, articles, academic papers, essays and more are available for your use. Having these on your hard disk and available to your word processor with its powerful search/find capabilities makes finding those elusive references a snap.

If you have a project in hand that needs research in what could loosely be called mainstream topics, say classical mythology or Mediterranean cooking, you are almost certain to find those topics out there. If your topic is a little more esoteric, say the works of a little-known fourteenth-century poet or keeping tarantulas as pets, it is still quite likely that some aficionados will have some information on a Website somewhere. In short, whatever your subject, you stand a good chance of finding material covering it on the Internet.

The immediacy of it all can be quite mesmerizing. Imagine you are in a large library researching your topic. You may come across a reference to a book that you would love to read, but the library does not have a copy. If you want to read it you may have to wait weeks for it to be ordered for you. On the Internet if you want it and it is available for download somewhere, you can have it now. Even if a dozen others have asked for it, it will still be available for you. No more waiting until the current user has returned it. Not only is research quicker, it is possible that you may look at information you would not have tried to get hold of in normal circumstances, because of the difficulties involved.

The Internet is never going to replace manual research. Whoa! Go back. Replace 'never going to' with 'not yet ready to'. The Internet is still in its absolute infancy. Think of a way it *could* be used and that is one way it *will* be used at a future date, if that way is advantageous.

There are few strict demarcations between means of getting at information from the Internet. Some research is better done on the Web and some is not. And some ways of searching for and retrieving information is an amalgam of both older-style programs and the newer Web browser.

At the end of this chapter is a short section on using CDs for research. It is not quite the Internet, but CDs can be a useful first source of reference material and many CDs have Internet links built in, thus extending their usefulness as a research tool. Two dictionary CD-ROMs are mentioned for no reason other than I like them!

Finally, remember copyright restrictions. It may seem obvious, but whatever you do, do not just cut-and-paste information you find. Someone, somewhere, will own the copyright to what you are reading. Use it only as a research source, not as work to plunder. (You will find more on copyright in Chapter 6.)

4.1 Reliable information

The previous caveats that came with seeking advice on the Internet apply to any research you may do. The value of the information is directly related to its accuracy and unless you are quite certain of the quality of the source you must be wary of its reliability.

There is a story, possibly apocryphal, of a professor lecturing a class on astronomy. Having delivered a reasoned explanation of the chances that intelligent life *may* exist elsewhere in the universe, he was interrupted by a student. 'Of course there are UFOs out there; it's all over the Internet!' Just because you can shout loudly and build a Website, it doesn't mean you are right.

Academic institutions, especially their library sites, are a fairly safe bet for accuracy. If you have dipped into an accessible area of a .edu or .ac.uk site and are looking at an undergraduate's Website – often signalled by a directory with a tilde followed by a name (e.g. /~sbrown/) – a little more care is needed than if you are looking at the part of the site run by the institution itself. A likely looking piece on anthropological research into New Guinea tribes may be an unmarked undergraduate's paper that is heading for a D minus grade, and so is your article on headhunters if you use the paper ingenuously. However, if the paper has a bibliography that links to other sites and papers, you may be able to use those to assess the first paper for accuracy or even use those sources themselves. You can also find subdirectories with 'faculty' in the name, e.g. www.mycollege. ac.uk/engl/faculty/~brown. These should be more reliable as they are pages put up by the faculty members who *should* be better informed than their students.

Use common sense in assessing value. If you find information wildly different from what you have already found, then, if not dismissive, at least be sceptical. If you are placing emphasis on having accurate dates for an event, then I would suggest it would be unwise to use just one source for the dates. Find other sources and compare dates for accuracy. At the risk of overstating the obvious, remember that no single source of information is totally reliable. Look at *where* you find it, *who* has written it, *when* it was written and *what* other sites it links to. Another way to describe this process is *Location, Author, Date* and *Links*.

4.2 Newsgroups

Making newsgroups work for you

The newsgroups you receive regularly are not your only source of information. When you have been subscribing to your writing newsgroup(s) for a few months it is easy to forget that there are thousands of newsgroups still out there.

If you have a project that needs research on a particular subject and that subject is covered by a newsgroup, why not subscribe? You can search for the newsgroup in all the previous ways suggested for finding writing groups. Members of newsgroups with nothing to do with writing should not be neglected. For example, subscribers to rec.aviation.military are bound to be interested in military aircraft so if you need information on this topic what do you have to lose by asking this group? If you have specific questions that you want to ask, then perhaps a search first on My Deja for past posts on that topic will either help find a useful newsgroup or answer the questions.

You can still ask members of your writing newsgroup if they either know anything about what you are researching or know of somewhere that you might find help. They may have re-searched the same topic themselves; after all they are writers just like you.

How 'netiquette' may limit your requests

Do not expect the members of a newsgroup to do all your work for you. If you are putting something together to write an arti-cle or a book that you expect to profit from, then there will be justifiable outrage if you expect others to hand over their own work for you to plunder.

If your subject is controversial then stand by for fireworks. One writer in a newsgroup asked for people with bad experiences of Alcoholics Anonymous (AA) to mail her with their 'AA, not booze, screwed up my life', stories, to be included in a book she had been commissioned to write. The group ignited and polarized into pro- and anti-AA factions. I gather that the writer was bombarded with mail, mostly flames. If she had at least given the impression that she was intending to produce a balanced work (whether she was or not), then perhaps the like-lihood of such an uproar would have been slighter. As it was, bubbles of rage were still occasionally rising months later.

Members are much more likely to share their experience with you if you make it plain that you are looking for resources to research yourself, rather than for packaged goods with all the work done. If you are seeking anecdotes for your own version of *Chicken Soup for the Soul*, then expect to pay cash for con-tributions – after all *Chicken Soup* does. Those writers are just like you; they want to be paid for their work. That does not stop them wanting to help; they remain a great resource for you, so ask for help and not finished copy, and you will get some great leads.

4.3 Universities, dictionaries and encyclopaedias

University Websites are usually only fully available to those with authorization, such as staff, students and accredited researchers. Some pages and files may be mirrored on other sites that are accessible. However, the parts of the sites that you can reach often contain a wealth of links to other, open, sites and can prove to be a good start for searching on a topic. Remember the top domain names for education sites and try different names for universities in order to access these sites. Oxford University is reached at **www.ox.ac.uk** for instance, Cornell at **www.cornell.edu**. You can search for 'university' as a wide search or 'ac.uk' on a search restricted to URLs for a long list of sites, for example.

A good place to find valuable information is in the public directories on university FTP servers. Their addresses can usually be guessed at if you cannot find them. Try 'ftp' before the Web address and look in pub or public directories. An address may finally look like ftp.ox.ac.uk/pub/ or ftp://ftp.ox.ac.uk/pub/ if using a browser. When reached via the Web, the FTP site will be presented by Internet Explorer in the same way as your hard disk directories in browser view (see Figure 4.1).

Librarians at universities maintain a list of Web reference sites and guarantee these sites for the authenticity of their information. They can be good sources for research. Try searching for 'Web reference sites' on a Web search engine – Excite yields particularly good results. Other sites have lists of links. An especially good one is www.britannica.com, containing a huge collection of links organized by category and selected by the editors of Britannica – highly recommended.

For an absolutely terrific site try **www.libraryspot.com**. This site will lead you to countless well-authenticated sites that will aid your research. Buried in the site itself are many pages of information that augment the sites referred to by the links. Best of all you can subscribe to a monthly newsletter that keeps you up to date with new reference sites. Despite the American orientation there is enough information here to satisfy anyone from anywhere. However, be aware that you will be led to some sites (for instance university libraries) that you cannot access without the appropriate authority (student password, course number etc.).

There are countless sites that access dictionaries and searching for 'dictionaries' or 'thesaurus' will yield many results, some of which will be book-selling sites, but some will take an input from you and come back with a definition or a selection of synonyms or antonyms. A new site on the Web is the complete *Oxford English Dictionary* (**www.oed.com**). This site gives access to the multi-volume set of books that is the bible of the English lexicographer. At present the site charges for access, but this may change along the model of other sites that began as fee-paying and then became free. You may even contribute words and sources of words to the dictionary. See **http://www.oed.com/public/readers/research.htm** for information.

Try a search for foreign language dictionaries. There are also translation sites, but their attempts at turning your prose into sparkling German or impeccable French usually fall short of perfection. There is some way to go before the Web replaces paper reference and human linguistic abilities in this regard.

Encyclopaedias are available on the Web. As a personal opinion, *Encyclopaedia Britannica*, found at the site given above, is one of the best. Once costing US$5 per month for a subscription, access to the whole encyclopaedia is now available free of charge. The site offers relevant Web links along with links to any articles that a search returns. These links lead both to sites where further information on the subject can be found and

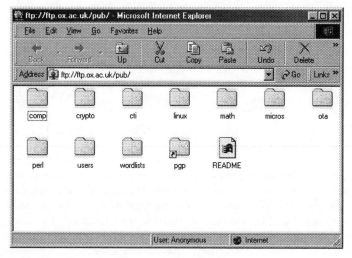

Figure 4.1 Internet Explorer presentation of an FTP site

also to commercial sites. If you search for something on popular music, for instance, links may lead you to sites selling CDs. Apparently it is the presence of these links that pay for the site – a small price for free availability of such a powerful reference library.

Two other good sites are **encarta.msn.com**, the online version of Microsoft's popular electronic encyclopaedia, and the concise *Columbia* at **www.encyclopedia.com**. A search for 'encyclopaedias' will give you a list of sites where reference works are available and sites that contain links to many encyclopaedia sites. Some sites charge a fee for full access, although here Britannica is showing a new way forward. The CIA has a site that opens its world fact-file to the public – you too can learn how they get things wrong so frequently. (See page 93 for CD encyclopaedias.)

If you are stuck for quotes with which to start the chapters of your latest book, **www.famous-quotations.com** will have some for you. Once again, try searching for 'quotes' or 'quotations' to find sites that interest you.

Not quite fitting into this section, but a Website that deserves exposure is Ask An Expert (**www.askanexpert.com**). This is a free service that offers answers to any question you might care to ask in the listed categories. Let us take a quick example.

At the site's home page you find a large selection of topics to choose from. You pick *Science/Technology*. This leads you to a page full of sub-categories where you choose *Physics*. On the physics page is a long list of previously asked questions and the answers provided. If you find your question there already then fine, if you do not you have the ability to ask your own question. This appears to be a neat idea and could be worth a try.

4.4 PDF files

Portable Document Format (PDF) files, created by the program Adobe Acrobat, are a way of presenting text and graphics in book form for display on a computer using a special reader program. They are more fully described in Chapter 5 on electronic publishing. One problem with PDF files is that the majority of search engines, apart from Google, only index HTML and text files, ignoring files in other formats such as

PDF. There is a wealth of information out there in PDF format if only you could find it and Adobe has started a search site that catalogues over a million PDF files in order for you to do just that.

Adobe's PDF is now pretty much the standard for distribution of electronic documents: widely used in academic circles, it makes distributing and sharing papers and reports easy. However, because of the lack of indexes for PDF files they are not readily accessible using normal search techniques. Finding an appropriate Website indexed by a search engine and then using a hyperlink on an HTML file on that site or knowing the exact location on the Web of the document was the only way to access such a file. Now Adobe's PDF Search Engine at **http://searchpdf.adobe.com/** makes these files accessible to you. The search engine holds summaries of more than a million online PDF documents. Because the PDF files themselves can

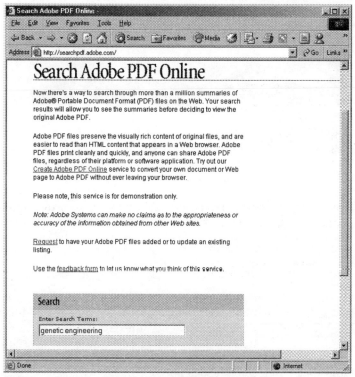

Figure 4.2 Adobe PDF search engine home page

be quite large (sometimes in the multi-megabyte range) clicking the links on the search results page doesn't automatically download the documents. A summary will be shown instead and the option to view online or download will be offered.

Imagine that your latest thriller requires your protagonist to be knowledgeable about genetic engineering. You would like to read up on the subject and wonder if there is any information out there that you might download. Let's try a search for PDF files of interest.

When you connect up to the Adobe PDF engine you are presented with the home page shown in Figure 4.2.

Typing 'genetic engineering' into the search box and clicking the 'Search' button leads you to the results page, shown in Figure 4.3. With the number of results totalling 6117 there must surely be some of interest to you.

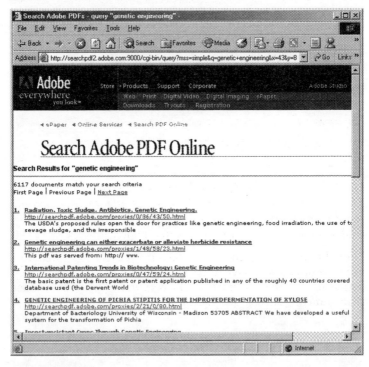

Figure 4.3 PDF search results page

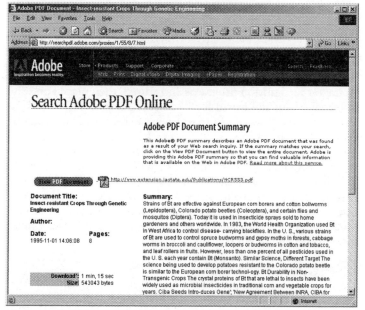

Figure 4.4 PDF summary

Paging down the first results page we come across a file on insect-resistant crops and genetic engineering. We click on the hyperlink and are led to the page shown in Figure 4.4.

Information on this page shows us a summary of the document, the size (about 530Kb) and the approximate download time with an average modem connection (1 minute 15 seconds). There is also a hyperlink that will take you directly to the document so that you can download it if you wish. To view the document after downloading you will require the Adobe reader – more on how to get this in Chapter 5.

Note that there is no guarantee that any of these files will be of use to you; you will have to check them out to see for yourself. But using Adobe PDF search is the best way to find them other than someone specifically telling you about them.

4.5 Gutenberg

Named after the fifteenth-century printer, the Gutenberg Project aims to convert all written text in archives and libraries into e-text – text readable by computer. The original stated aim was to give away 10,000 e-texts to 100,000,000 readers by the end of 2001. I believe that they are short of the number of e-texts, but have reached the target reader number.

Printed text is scanned into computers, run through optical character recognition programs and edited, then placed on servers throughout the world for free access. If you do not possess a copy of *The Wizard of Oz* and need it for a project, you can download it from any one of several hundred sites as a plain text file readable by any computer. Download the complete works of Shakespeare and use your word processor's ability to search for text if you want a quick way to find a passage you only half remember. The Bible is available if you need a quote to support a stance you have taken in your latest article. All the books in the Gutenberg Project are freely available and can be downloaded and stored on your own computer as a permanent reference if you so require. The original copyright to the majority of works has expired, but they are subject to some copyright restrictions – details on the Gutenberg site. Copyright is further discussed in Chapter 6.

You will not find the latest Tom Clancy book in Gutenberg, neither will you find that bestseller on Stalingrad that came out recently and costs £29.99 in your local bookstore. The majority of books available are old classics, but it is nice to have access to them.

A minor caveat here is that all the work is voluntary and the texts can suffer from typos caused by insufficient proofreading of the output from the optical character recognition programs used to convert the scanned pages into plain text. Despite the protestations from the Gutenberg team, there are misprints in some of the texts.

The main Gutenberg site can be reached at **http:// www.gutenberg.net/** where you will find links to indexes of books already converted to e-text and lists of forthcoming titles. If you find this site slow to access, then a simple search will return many other sites where this information can be found.

The Gutenberg Project alone is a good reason for connecting to the Internet; it is a vast storehouse of literature that is growing all the time.

4.6 E-mail lists

Getting information

If you have been a regular contributor to your list(s) for some time, you should be able to ask for research help with no problem. A lively list with many regulars will have a surprising number of people on it who have similar interests to you and an equally surprising number who have wildly different interests. From both camps you will get information on research sources and maybe even some direct information. Those with similar interests will probably give you sources that you are definitely going to like and those with dissimilar interests may well point you in directions that would have never occurred to you, but could still prove useful.

Remember the limitations of search engines; all the engines put together index at best less than 50 per cent of the Web. Some estimates put it at about 20 per cent. You will find many sites of interest when browsing. These sites may or may not have relevance to your current research, but if you find them of possible use to you then bookmark them. There is nothing more frustrating than to find and then lose a site of interest, and at a later date realize you need it, but cannot find it with a search. You can share these finds with your list members and they, in turn, will share their serendipitous discoveries with you. You could be amazed at how many sites the hundreds of writers on your various lists and newsgroups will know of, sites that may never be catalogued by search engines.

An incidental observation here is that browsers have ways in which you can organize bookmarks. My advice is – organize them! A simple system of filing the bookmarks under appropriate categories (research, writing, music, newspapers – whatever you choose – and sub-categories within them) will save you much work when you are looking for one you need. To begin with you will find it easy to cope with a straightforward list, but as your collection grows the list will get longer. Scrolling through it looking for that site you know you bookmarked can be tedious. The time to organize is early on, when you can learn the discipline. This is a case when I wish I always took my own advice! I still find myself devoting the odd half-hour or so getting my bookmark list back into some kind of shape.

The same rules apply here as apply to newsgroups. Look for sources, not completed work. Crudely put, your list members should be cows as a source of milk, not beef. It is a renewable resource for you if used properly.

Using feedback

If you look on your list members as milk sources, do not forget that cows need feeding. Give to the list when you can. As previously mentioned, the more you help others on your list, the more they will be prepared to help you. Be generous with your sources if you expect them to be forthcoming with theirs.

There is nothing the list likes more than to hear of your successes. If your researches lead you to a seam of gold, then tell them. If your book, article or whatever, written with their help sells, then let them know about it and let them know the value of their input. They will love it.

4.7 Standard e-mail

Interviews

E-mail is a great way to communicate. So many people are now connected to the Internet that e-mail is a valid substitute for the postal service, or snail-mail as it is often called on the Web.

Do you need to interview somebody for an article? If they have an e-mail address then you may arrange a face-to-face interview that way. You might e-mail a list of questions to prepare your interviewee; you could even conduct the interview entirely by e-mail – people on the other side of the world to you suddenly become available for interview. It is best to be restrained in your e-mails when interviewing this way. Ask for an interview first and then mail only a few questions at a time; you can always send more. And stop before the interviewee gets bored with answering your mail; you may want to interview them at a later date. If you pretend that you are carrying out an interview on the phone with long delays between questions and answers, you will not go wrong.

Does a piece you are writing contain facts of which you are

unsure? If you know a reliable authority on the subject in question, an e-mail could elicit a fuller answer than a phone call – cheaper too if the call would be long distance or international. The reply could also include links to other authorities if your correspondent desires.

Do you need copyright permissions, or perhaps confirmation that a passage you are going to quote is not in copyright? An e-mail to author or publisher could bring a prompt response and a printed record of a e-mail reply giving express permission should be fine for your own publisher/editor when he or she checks copyrights in your work.

E-mail address searches

The biggest problem with e-mail communication is finding the right e-mail address. Here search engines can come to the rescue again. Several engines offer e-mail address searches, but the results are not reliable. Companies can often be found in Yellow Pages engines – these are given as links on many search engine sites – but individuals can be hard to track down.

Yahoo! People Search at **people.yahoo.com** is a good engine for this type of search. Others can be tracked down using your trusty search engine techniques. They include: InfoSpace (**www.infospace.com**), Switchboard (**www.switchboard.com**), and WhoWhere? (**www.whowhere.lycos.com**) just for starters. The page on SearchIQ reached at **www.zdnet.com/searchiq/ subjects/people** will offer a long list of ways to search for a name and address, both Internet and real. FerretSoft (**www.zdnet.com/ferret/index.html**) has a good program called EmailFerret that is used from your browser to search for addresses. Common sense is needed in winnowing the returns down to ones likely to be correct. For example, out of several returns for a search on the author Terry Pratchett, there is one address given as **Tpratchett@unseen.demon.co.uk**. As he is a British author who writes about a universe that includes a place called the Unseen University, there is good chance – note *good*, not 100 per cent – that it is the correct one.

If you have problems finding someone's e-mail address:

♦ Phone or write and ask them directly. This negates the advantage of e-mail for the first communication, but leaves you with the address for any further need.

- If you know that your target individual works at a company with e-mail, try sending e-mail to them name@theircompany. Names are often in the form firstname_lastname or initial_lastname where an underline symbol joins the names, or the names may be just run into each other with no joining symbol. Mail that cannot be delivered should be returned to you (known as *bounced mail*) with an explanation of why it could not be delivered – 'nobody at this address' if you have it wrong, for instance.

- Publishers, who can be found in Yellow Pages, may give out an e-mail address for an author whom they publish. The author's details or preface in one of his or her books may give an address.

- Someone on your trusty e-mail lists or an appropriate newsgroup may know.

The Internet is waiting for someone to come up with an easy and completely reliable way to look up e-mail addresses. Large sums of money await the inventor.

4.8 Internet Relay Chat

Just as you would be foolish to bet your life on what you heard someone say on CB radio, you would be equally silly to base a book on the kind of hearsay that flies around on IRC. It is possible to pick up some pointers to resources that can be examined at leisure, but not much more.

ISP forums

Forums in the main are no better and no worse than newsgroups. Some forums have guest appearances where writers will be on the Net to answer questions and generally chat about their work. If the writer is popular it can be difficult to get in to ask a question – which is done through a moderator who can censor questions if necessary. If a writer is on a guest appearance, you may be able to put a question that fills in some research for you or may learn something about writing techniques from the chatter.

Time zone differences can be problematic. Most guest appearances take place at times favourable to the US subscribers, leaving the rest of the world participating at what is, to them, an inconvenient time of day or night.

4.9 CD-ROMs

Extending research from CD-ROMs to the Internet

The promise of an encyclopaedia on a disk has been realized, but how well are these volumes implemented? The answer is quite well and not so well. One useful facility provided by CDs is that links embedded in articles lead either to other relevant or complementary articles on the CD or to Websites that can take you further into the topic you are reading. Here is a quick summary of some of the more popular CDs, a far from exhaustive selection.

Encarta

Microsoft appears to have cornered the popular market yet again with its Encarta CD. The encyclopaedia is good and is available in a 'world' version with slightly less bias towards America. The articles leave something to be desired if you need in-depth research, but searching for relevant articles is easy. For research purposes there is, perhaps, too much emphasis on multi-media and not enough on text. Updates are available on the Web and there are many links to sites relating to articles. It is now available on DVD.

Encyclopaedia Britannica

Sold in two forms, the basic and the multi-media version, this is relatively expensive, but is the ultimate in currently available reference CDs. Containing all the articles from the many Britannica volumes and a dictionary as well, this is definitely a fine resource to use as a starting point for research. Many articles have hyperlinks to sites on the Web that can extend their research value. These links are not guaranteed to work due to the changing nature of the Web, but the Britannica Website (**www.britannica.com**) offers updates to articles and links.

Microsoft Bookshelf

This quick reference gem offers *Chambers Dictionary*, *Roget's Thesaurus*, the *Bloomsbury Treasury of Quotations*, the *Concise Encarta Encyclopaedia*, and Harrap's *Concise English–German– English* and *English–French–English* dictionaries. There is also a section that contains links to major Websites. It presents a selection of keywords in alphabetical order that are expandable to subsections. Each subsection has a link and a short description of the site. It is more of a writer's aid than a research tool, but a valuable resource none the less.

Penguin Hutchinson Reference Library

A decidedly British-oriented library for a change. The CD contains the *Longman Dictionary*, the *Hutchinson Encyclopaedia*, *Roget's Thesaurus*, *The Compact Chronology of World History*, *The Penguin Dictionary of Quotations*, *Usage and Abusage* and *The Helicon Book of Days*. This CD gives good, if limited, research facilities and provides an excellent reference source.

Compton's Complete Reference Collection

Another good reference selection. *Compton's Concise Encyclopaedia*, *The World Almanac & Book of Facts*, *Webster's New World Dictionary and Thesaurus*, *Merriam-Webster's Concise Handbook for Writers*, an atlas, *Merriam-Webster's Geographical Dictionary*, *Columbia Home Medical Guide* are all included. There is also an Internet directory listing some 4000 links.

Finally, here are two CD dictionaries that you may like. They do not have links to the Web; they are merely mentioned out of interest.

The Concise Oxford Dictionary

Exceptionally well laid out, this CD can be tied in to Microsoft Word for easy reference. Small, this dictionary is none the less comprehensive in nature. While it will not supplant your trusty, large, paper dictionary, it can be useful for quick reference as you work on your word processor.

The New Shorter Oxford English Dictionary

This is a fantastic CD with more on it than you will probably ever need. There are four different kinds of search you may carry out: simple, index, full and special. The 'simple' is exactly what it says. The 'index' offers headword, derivative and abbreviation searches with headword subdivided into parts of speech, label and date if you so require. The label gives dozens of categories from Accountancy to Zoology, Botany to Medicine. The date enables a search for words first used, in use and last used in a selected period. Phrases and compound words, uses and references and other forms of words can be searched. Under 'full' you may search for etymology, definition and quotations referred to and under 'special' anagrams, rhymes and phonetics can be located. This one could certainly supplant your paper version.

There are many other CD-ROMs on the market, wildly varying in price. If you are interested in discovering the best of the new CDs as they appear, monthly computer magazines often run comparative reviews. Most of these magazines have Websites and surprising amounts of the magazine contents are available for reading on the Net, usually free of charge. Try the search tip on company names in URLs to find them, carry out a complete search on an engine or read the editorial masthead in the printed magazine for the address.

It is worth checking over the computer magazines at your news seller. Both the computer and the Internet oriented magazines have 'free' cover-mounted CDs. Many useful reference works can be obtained for the cost of the magazine. Even if the encyclopaedia, dictionary or whatever is an older version than the market leader, or has been supplanted by a new edition from the same company, it may still be worth having for your reference library. You need to be aware that the older versions may have some broken links to Websites, however.

Another type of CD that is useful for reference, if not exactly research, is the library collection. These CDs are numerous, relatively cheap and contain many books in the form of e-text. Programs on the disk enable easy text searches to be carried out. Many books are from the Gutenberg Project and buying CDs containing many e-texts – rather than downloading the files over the Internet – can save you time and cut your phone bills.

4.10 Online newspapers

Newspapers, current and archived, can be good places to research information. Published articles have been researched by journalists with all the resources of their papers behind them and all their contacts to help them, so why not read those that are relevant to anything you may be writing and see if they can help.

A list of over 5000 online newspapers from all over the world can be found at **http://reporter.umd.edu/newspapers.htm**, another huge list is at **http://www.thepaperboy.com/**. The papers run the whole gamut from small town press to big city and nationwide newspapers. You can select the newspaper of your choice from one of these lists or you can use sites that are designed to make broader searches a little easier.

Some addresses are given in the Appendices, but try searching for good sites yourself. Try 'online newspapers' or 'online newspaper archives' in one of the meta-search engines discussed in Chapter 3 and try the sites that are returned until you come across one that suits you.

Let us look at an example of a search on newspapers, which will only scratch the surface of what you can do.

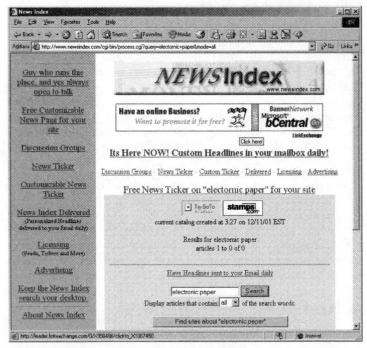

Figure 4.5 News Index home page

Imagine you are writing an article on the new electronic publishing process and would like to see what the press has written in order to get some background information. You have heard the term 'electronic paper' and wonder what information there might be about it. News Index (**http://www.newsindex.com/**) is a site that links to sites which have a news search or an online database of archived newspapers. You start there, where you find the page shown in Figure 4.5.

You type in 'electronic paper' as your search term and press the 'Search' button. The results page (Figure 4.6) shows over 1500 articles referring to 'electronic paper', but scrolling down the first page of results leads you to an article that looks as if it might be both relevant and of interest (Figure 4.7).

As an article title, 'Quality leap for e-paper developers' seems to fit the bill and the short extract, actually part of the first paragraph of the article, leads you to the decision that you would like to read it.

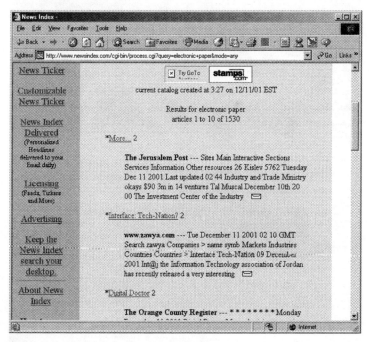

Figure 4.6 News Index search results

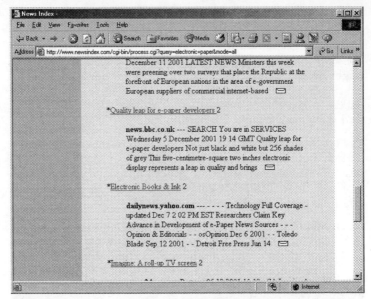

Figure 4.7 Relevant article on results page

Figure 4.8 Electronic paper article

Clicking on the underlined hyperlink leads you directly to the website containing this article, which happens to be the BBC website (**http://www.bbc.co.uk/**) – a site that is well worth bookmarking as it contains a wealth of useful background material for a writer (Figure 4.8).

With over 1500 articles to browse through you probably think that you have enough background to be going on with, but in case you feel the need for more, we'll have a look at another source of information.

The site **http://mypage.bluewin.ch/a-z.cusipage/newsarch.html** gives access to several news-search engines as well as many US and world newspaper archives. We'll try the general archives and the default search engine, News Yahoo!, for another search on electronic paper (Figure 4.9).

Scrolling down the page of results, which number over 100, we come across an interesting article on Philips Electronics (Figure 4.10). Clicking, once again, on the underlined hyperlink we are taken to the news section of Yahoo!, where we can read the article in question (Figure 4.11).

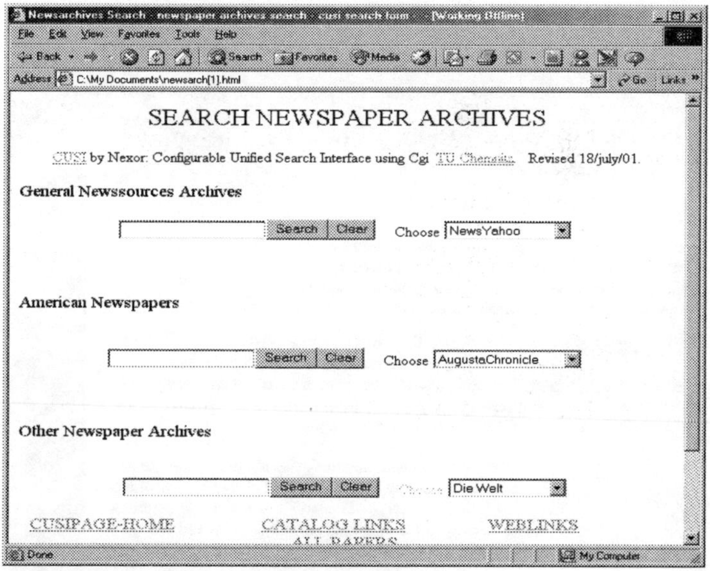

Figure 4.9 Newspaper archive search

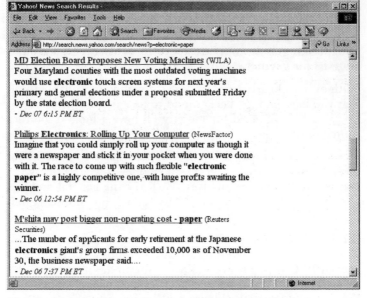

Figure 4.10 Newspaper archive search results

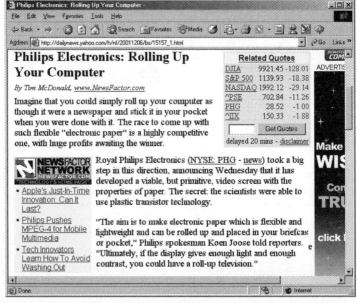

Figure 4.11 Philips Electronics article

The articles we have found may not be of any use to us or we might want to see some more. In this case we can keep on looking in News Index or the archive at **mypage.bluewin.ch** with different search terms, or try another archive such as **www.journalismnet.com/archives/**, or look at the results that a search engine returns. If and when we do find an article of use we can easily copy it and save it on hard disk in a clippings file; a far neater way to keep articles of interest than using scissors and a box to store physical cuttings. And of course you may find something online in a newspaper you would never see otherwise. How many of us regularly take the *Hindustan Times* for instance? It has an online presence (**www.hindustantimes.com**).

Summary

* Be wary of the reliability of information you obtain. Examine the source, try not to rely on only one source and cross-reference if possible. Remember Location, Author, Date and Links as a test.

* Don't neglect newsgroups as a source of information.

* Your new friends on your e-mail lists can help. Try them.

* Don't expect others to do *all* the work for you.

* Use libraries and university sites for reliable information.

* Use Gutenberg. You can even contribute if you have some spare time!

* CDs can be useful as a first source of reference and often contain many useful Internet links.

* Remember that newspaper archives can be a great source of background information.

Exercises

1 Think of a project you might wish to undertake – writing an article, a short story, a novel, a non-fiction book etc. Map out the areas that need background research. See how much of that research you can carry out on the Internet trying both laser and shotgun techniques.

2 Find a current item of news and see how much you can retrieve on it from the Internet. Try news sources from various countries and see how their 'slant' on the news varies.

3 Using the same news item as above, try to find any parallel items of news from past newspaper/magazine archives. See if you can write an original article from the comparison.

4 Search for and download a PDF article of interest to you. Remember you will need to download the Acrobat reader first.

5 Find a friend who has access to e-mail and practise interviewing them for an article on their hobby/interest.

6 Search the magazine racks for free CD-ROMs with reference titles. When you use them try the links that they provide and see what sources they use for reference. If you find any sources of use to you, bookmark them.

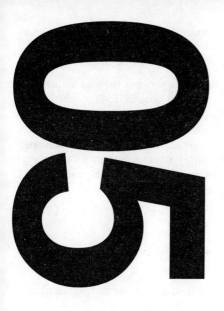

05

electronic publishing

In this chapter you will learn

- what e-publishing is
- how to avoid the pitfalls of publishing

This chapter aims to help you to find new ways to publish your work and offer guidelines and advice to ensure that you will not be 'stung' when you do entrust your work to cyberspace.

The word publishing may bring to a writer's mind a vision of paper, presses, agents, editors and (hooray!) royalty cheques. The process seems simple: write something, mail it to a book or magazine publisher, receive an acceptance letter and wait for publication and payment. First serial or volume rights have been sold – at least for the country in which the article, story or book is published – and, in an ideal world, the process can be repeated in another country.

Electronic publishing is not necessarily the same. It could consist of:

◆ Publishing your own Website.

◆ Contributing to an electronic magazine.

◆ Publishing a book either for reading online or for distribution on disk.

◆ Using the Internet as a route to 'normal', paper publication.

There are problems of rights to consider. People on the Internet are infamous for ignoring copyright, either wilfully or through ignorance, and legal protection for work published on the Net is not yet fully established. It is generally accepted that copyright resides with the author of a work when it has been written, without a requirement to register the copyright (see Chapter 6 for more details). However, publication rights such as first UK serial rights are not so clear-cut.

There are also people out there who want your money and are not particularly squeamish about the ways they use to get it. The Internet is no different from the real world in this respect, the methods may differ slightly, but the end result of a confidence trick will be exactly the same. A major difference is the difficulty of policing the Net and of catching up with the conmen and scam-runners.

5.1 Web pages

Publishing your own Website

Why should you need your own Website? There could be several reasons, but if you are a writer who wants to be paid for doing something you find enjoyable, then advertising your skills will probably be the main reason. Your Website has a potential audience of millions, although realistically you should think in terms of hundreds unless you have something incredibly special to offer.

A writer's Website needs to be a showcase for the writer's work and for any other related, and sellable, expertise such as editing, translation or proofreading, for example. Unless you can dream up a way to make visitors to your site pay you for the privilege of reading your work or persuade companies to advertise on your (hopefully) highly visited pages, a Website, of itself, is not going to earn you money. If you can build a site that somehow attracts visitors, who see your work, are impressed and seek you out for employment or buy your already published books, you may earn money from it. The chances of this happening are remote. If you do build your own site, do not have over-high expectations.

You may wish to pass on your knowledge and use articles you have written on writing problems. In this case you need to provide links to other sites and articles. There are plenty of sites that have been published with this aim in mind, so if you are doing it for this reason you will need to provide something unique that the others do not. Only this way will you attract visitors.

There is neither the space in this book nor the expertise on the author's part to guide you through the physical process of designing a Website. There are specialist books on the subject of design and ISPs to guide you through the process of uploading your finished site. *HTML: Publishing on the World Wide Web* by Mac Bride in the *Teach Yourself* series is a good starting point. If you decide a Website is what you need, then consult these sources of help. A look at the following well-designed sites may give you some idea of what is needed for self-promotion and how a Website can be more than 'wordy' advertising, actually entertaining the reader as well as 'pushing' books.

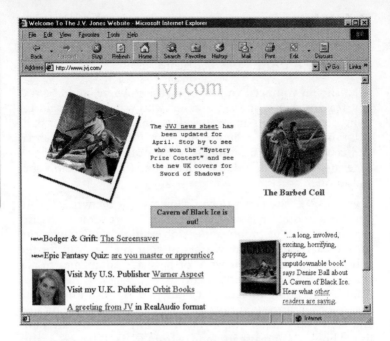

Figure 5.1 Home page of J.V. Jones' Website

Katherine Neville's Website can be found at **www. katherineneville.com**. She has published the books *The Eight*, *A Calculated Risk* and *The Magic Circle*.

J.V. Jones, author of *The Book of Words* trilogy, *The Barbed Coil*, and a new fantasy trilogy beginning with *The Cavern of Black Ice*, is at **www.jvj.com** .

Loss of rights may be a problem here if you wish to sell your work to a normal publisher after using it on your site. Some consider that publication on the Web amounts to the use of first serial rights and you may find it difficult to sell anything that has been so exposed. This potential problem should be resolved in future.

Some people will take your work and put it up on their own Website. They may pay you a small amount for it, or may take it as a favour, or they may even lift it from other sources without your knowledge. Rights are again at issue here.

5.2 Ezines and magazines

An ezine is simply a magazine that publishes on the Web. There are many and they cover several genres, although science fiction seems to be a staple. There are two types of ezine, ones that publish a Website that you visit to read, and ones that you may subscribe to and which are then e-mailed to you. The e-mail version is similar to the newsletters described in Chapter 2.

The following is a site that offers lists of ezines. A Web search for ezines will return others.

http://www.etext.org/ is an e-text archive displaying:

- Electronic periodicals from the professional to the personal.
- Political ezines, essays, and home pages of political groups.
- Publications of amateur authors.
- Mainstream and off-beat religious texts.
- An eclectic mix of mostly amateur poetry.
- The archive formerly hosted at **quartz.rutgers.edu**.

The ezines themselves vary greatly in quality, type, subject matter and frequency of publication, and also cover a broad band between professional and totally amateur presentation. Some will pay for contributions – usually small sums, but sometimes up to US$250. Some will not pay anything.

It is not unknown for submissions to ezines to be published without paying, informing or sometimes even acknowledging the author. Writers have found work published by ezines to which they have never submitted and also published with unauthorized cuts and editing.

Good ezines are unlikely to want a piece that has been published elsewhere on the Web. This may include work put up on your own Website.

Newsletters are a source of ezine writing opportunities. Most have lists of specific requirements that have been picked up from the Internet by either the newsletter editors or informed contributors.

Arts & Letters Daily is an excellent example of a good online magazine. Full of ideas, criticisms and debate, it can be found at **http://www.aldaily.com**. It also has dozens of articles, links to

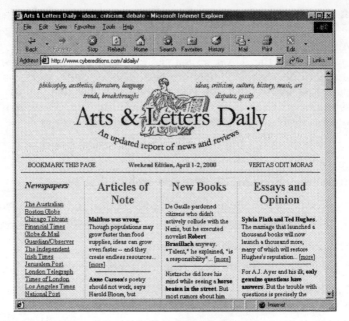

Figure 5.2 Top of the *Arts & Letters Daily* page

many newspapers, magazines, columnists, journals, news services, reviews and more. This publication will do more than just keep you up to date with literary affairs, it will also give you ideas for writing new articles and background for articles you have under way.

If you want to start your own ezine there is help available on the Web. One starting point is *EzineUniversity Journal* (**http://www.ezineuniversity.com**).

5.3 Mass market magazines

There are usually Websites for the major magazines found at your newsagent. Few in the UK will accept articles by e-mail at the time of writing. This will change. Indeed it is changing in America, where more magazines are putting up pages on their Websites specifically for writers, giving writers' guidelines as well as accepting contributions by e-mail. If you are an article writer, look out in future for a much easier route to publication in your target magazine. It will make the world magazine market far more accessible than it is today, doing away with postal reply coupons and exorbitant airmail expenses.

If and when you find a magazine that will take your article by e-mail – either for publication on the Web or on the newsstand – there are a few points to remember.

Send your covering letter in the same format as you would if you were using snail mail – return address (snail mail and e-mail address), date, what rights you are offering to sell (if you usually include something like 'first British serial rights', for instance), Dear 'name of the editor to whom you are submitting', yours sincerely or whatever ending you normally use, your name and so on. Editors still like to see a large degree of formality and although it is becoming more common in general e-mail not to bother with any capitals, and to be lax with grammar and punctuation, it will not go down well to be so relaxed and informal in the case of a covering letter.

Follow any instructions that the magazine gives for format of the article. They may require single-spaced text with double-spacing between paragraphs, for instance, or no indented paragraphs. Whatever it is, do it. If there is no guidance, then the above format is usually acceptable.

Unless specifically requested *do not* send your article as an attachment. Most e-mail programs will allow you to send a document as, for example, a Microsoft Word .doc file. The idea of sending your work this way may be attractive as it preserves your fancy fonts and formatting, but because of the danger of viruses that can be put into attached files, many companies will automatically reject attachments without opening them (see Chapter 6 on security). It is hard enough getting work published as it is without courting rejection in this way.

If using the word processor built in to your mail program, remember to set the word-wrap to about 75 characters width or less – 70 is probably safest. If you use a program like Word or WordPerfect, save the file as a text file, import it into your mail program and ensure that it is merged into the e-mail as in-line text – see your program manual for help. An article that

breaks lines, leaving a word or two hanging is so hard to read that
your work will probably be rejected without being read if

it is
mangled in this way. A long article will almost certainly
be rejected.
It really is hard work reading long passages split up like this.

If you are having problems working out whether or not your
mail is turning out this way for other readers then temporarily
subscribe to the alt.test newsgroup, send off a sample paragraph or two and wait for it to come back to you on the
newsgroup – it could take up to a day. When you see the result
in your newsreader you should see if you are doing it right.

Do not forget that all the normal rules of submission still apply
– following any guidelines, keeping the number of words right
and obeying all the other rules that you have learnt already in
your writing career.

Just because e-mail is cheap and easy do not badger the editor
with e-mails asking if your work has been accepted when you
have not had a reply in a week. Treat the article-out and ac-
ceptance/rejection-letter-back cycle as you would when using
the postal service.

Remember the problems that may arise with previous publication on the Web. The magazine may consider the first rights
already sold and reject work for this reason.

The Writers' & Artists' Yearbook (published by A & C Black),
The Writer's Handbook (Macmillan) in the UK, and the US
publication *Writer's Market* (Writers' Digest Books) now all
show e-mail addresses and Websites for magazines and publishers who have them. As time passes these writers' reference
books will doubtless become more Internet oriented.

Here is a small selection of sites that may be of interest.

www.awoc.com
The Writer's Place offers a free searchable database of over 650
writers' guidelines of paying markets.

www.publist.com/
Offers a worldwide, searchable database of 150,000 magazines
and 8000 newspapers.

www.writersdigest.com/guidelines/index.htm
The *Writer's Digest* Big List of Guidelines. A database of over
1500 magazine and publishers' writer submission guidelines.

www.writersweekly.com

A newsletter with many paying markets listed.

www.writerswrite.com/guidelines/

A large writer submission guideline database that is searchable by magazine name and keyword.

www.inscriptionsmagazine.com/

Inscriptions magazine has a page of paying markets looking for specific articles. The page is updated regularly.

5.4 Collaboration

There may come a time in your writing career when you feel that you either just cannot produce a piece of work the way you would like or that you feel another input would turn what you have already written into something better. This might be the time for collaboration.

Your time in the communities of writing newsgroups and lists should give you a good idea of who could be the right person to ask to join in any collaborative effort. You will, after a time, know who has what interests that might fit into your idea for a project, whose writing skills you believe to be up to the task, whom you think will stick with a job to the end and not abandon it half finished and, perhaps most important, who you will personally relate to best.

Some writers' lists have collaborative stories going on. Initially a paragraph is written that sets the tone and in turn, by a pre-arranged rota, someone else will contribute a paragraph. Slowly the story builds up, owned by no one individual and with its path wandering wherever it will. As a writing exercise it is popular with some and not others. As a way to a complete story it is wildly variable in outcome. However, it may give you an idea who collaborates well, using the story line to push the paragraph they contribute rather than dragging the story line off in some agenda-driven direction of their own.

If you are stuck and just cannot find a collaborator then advertising your requirement on a newsgroup may help. This could be on a writers' newsgroup or, at a pinch, even on a newsgroup that is relevant to the subject of your project. Be aware that if you choose the second course you are not guaranteed to find someone who is a writer, just someone who might know a lot about the particular project subject. In this case you might be wiser to think in terms of using them for research rather than collaboration.

A collaborative effort is almost perfect for the Internet, second only to personal contact. Your collaborator will probably belong to more than one newsgroup/list that you do not belong to and so will have access to different writers for any research assistance – the same works for you and your different groups. The speed and cheapness of e-mail allow full texts of the collaboration to be passed backwards and forwards after additions or amendments.

The ability of mailer programs to send attachments – that is, a non-plain-text file (document, spreadsheet, audio clip, program, etc.) that travels with your normal e-mail – means that you can use the abilities of modern word processors to mark amendments in text so they are easily seen and then send the word-processed document to your collaborator. No longer are you stuck with the tedious task of marking in some way the parts you have altered before you send the file in plain text. No longer are you forced to pore over pages seeking these markings to check what your collaborator has altered. Your word processor does it for you.

You will need to be running the same word processor to enable this to work best. It will also be to your advantage to be using the same, up-to-date version. If Amanda is collaborating with Brian and Amanda uses WordPerfect while Brian uses Word, the files *are* convertible from one format to another with no loss of textual detail, but the steps of conversion will almost certainly lose the marks that indicated the recent amendments and possibly even the formatting of headings and so on.

File formats change as program versions change, too. Word 2 cannot read Word 97 (neither can read Word 2000) without a filter that converts the format. There are 'bells and whistles' in the newer versions that the older versions cannot use even after conversion – from Word 2000 to Word 2, for instance.

If you cannot reasonably use the same program – they are expensive to buy and owning several is not an option for most of us – it may still be possible to see amendments. Some word processors can do this for you. In Word you can open the old and the amended documents and tell the program to Track Changes. It will then highlight any changes for you. If this facility is not available in your word processor you will need another strategy.

You may need to come to some agreement as to how you will mark plain text files passed back and forth to show what amendments have been made – other than new additions at the end of the text, which should be obvious. Your word processor can be used to search for these marks: <NI> for newly inserted, <ALT> for a suggested alteration and whatever else you want to agree to, depending on your needs.

Remember, even if you are using different word processors, documents in their word-processed format can still be passed to and fro as attachments, as long as you both have the appropriate filters with your own programs to change the file format into something readable. Bear in mind that the fonts, layout and other niceties may not translate well – unexpected effects are not uncommon – so it could pay to keep the layouts as simple as possible. The time to worry over layout is after the project is completed.

An absolute essential is that you must agree on what file is the master copy, that is to say the one on which modifications can be made. Only one person should make alterations to the master at any one time and this should be the file passed back and forth. If you want to alter or add something when your collaborator is working on the master then do it in an extra file or scribble it on a piece of paper – whatever you do, *do not* alter the copy of the master that you have. If you do, confusion will reign supreme and Murphy, eponymous owner of the famous law, will win again. And don't forget to back up your work.

5.5 Publishing

There are four main types of publishing, both in the normal way and on the Internet.

Standard

In standard publishing your work is sold as a manuscript. The publisher does everything necessary to edit, produce and market it and pays you royalties on copies sold. The royalties will probably be around the 10–15 per cent mark for hardback sales and 6–10 per cent for softback. The author bears no costs of production other than any agreed by negotiable contract. If you pick up a book in your local bookseller it is almost certain to have been produced this way.

E-mail may help you contact publishers and their Websites may give you some guidance as to whether or not your work might be something that they would publish. The sites I have looked at appear to be more for laying out the publisher's wares than for offering a new route for would-be authors to communicate. In the main you would probably do better to use the time-honoured means of communication, at least when attempting to arouse a publisher's interest in your work.

A new departure by the publisher Macmillan is something that it calls AuthorNET (**www.macmillan.co.uk**). This is a Website for its authors that is accessible only by password. The site gives the names, telephone numbers and e-mail addresses of many people within the company that its authors may need to contact. There are plans to add contracts, royalty statements, book marketing plans and other information on authors' books. This is definitely a step in the right direction for improving electronic communications in what is still very much a paper-oriented industry.

Self-publishing

Self-publishing requires you to bear all costs. You can put design, printing and everything else out to tender, getting the best price you can, but bearing the expense and being responsible for the organization and synchronization of the different steps in the process. Marketing, storage, selling, etc. are all down to you and can become expensive. The advantage is that you keep 100 per cent of the proceeds when your work is sold. Bearing 100 per cent of the financial risks entitles you to this.

This can be a honourable route to publishing your work. Plenty of famous authors have done it, mostly before they became well known. Walt Whitman published *Leaves of Grass* this way, for instance. Some self-published books have been taken over by large publishing houses.

It entails hard work, large capital outlay and financial risk. The Internet can help in contacting printers, editors and designers to enable you to get the best deals for your money – but remember it is still early days and not all companies will be on the Web yet. When it comes to marketing you would be foolish to rely on electronic advertising to the exclusion of other means, but marketing and promoting your book over the Internet can be a good way to generate sales.

Send press releases pushing your book to every ezine and newsletter you can find. Start your own newsletter. Try the big online dealers like Amazon and bol.com – they may not be interested, but what have you got to lose? Search for book clubs online that might take your work. Set up a Website that extols its virtues, gives extracts to entice, mentions your promotional signings and tours, and most importantly offers a way to buy it. In short, use every device you can think of to put your name and book before the public eye.

An excellent source for information on the whole process of book production that you will find useful if you are thinking of self-publishing is *Books A to Z*, found at **http:// www.booksatoz.com**. When you have finished writing and

115

electronic publishing 05

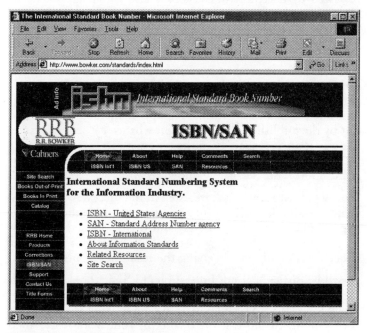

Figure 5.3 ISBN home page

designing it there is even a Website where you can get an ISBN number for it: **http://www.bowker.com/standards/index.html** and, in the UK, **http://www.whitaker.co.uk**.

Subsidy

Subsidy publishing is a joint partnership between publisher and author. Some costs – usually printing and binding – are borne by the author, some – often editing, storage and marketing – are borne by the publisher. The payment to the author is in the form of royalties, but, because of the financial involvement on the author's part, these royalties are higher than in standard publishing.

While there is an incentive for the publisher to promote your book – after all they take a cut of the proceeds of any sales – it is not as great an incentive as that faced by the standard publisher, who sees no return at all if there are no sales. Whatever claims a subsidy publisher may make, booksellers are reluctant to stock subsidy-published books and they are unlikely to be reviewed by decent critics. There is also the danger of being cheated by unscrupulous publishers (see below under *Scams*).

Vanity

Vanity publishing is just a way for an author to get a manuscript turned into a bound book. The author pays for everything. You will have to accept the publisher's designs, layout and book format. No editing, storage or marketing is carried out by the publisher. They will print whatever is sent in exactly the way it arrives, apart from the typographical errors that they will introduce, unless you pay them or someone they recommend more cash (see below under *Scams*).

Vanity publishers are less interested in the success of your work than subsidy publishers. Once you have paid for the printing, their connection with you ends and their financial interest is in getting as much money as possible out of you before the process ends with you receiving the result of the print run.

It will be difficult, if not impossible, to find a bookseller willing to stock a vanity-published book. It will be equally unlikely for a critic to be interested in even looking at it, let alone reviewing it. In short, if the quality of your work is not good enough for a standard publisher or even a subsidy publisher and you are not prepared for the hassle of self-publication you are likely to end up with a garage full of books you cannot sell.

A vanity publisher who tells you that your work is guaranteed to make money is correct, but he, not you, makes the money.

Scams

What a nasty, money-grubbing world we live in! Because of this the newsgroup alt.writing.scams is a good group to consider for your subscriber list. It is not highly active, but is where news of new scams, or old ones with a new twist, is often first posted. Visit My Deja for past postings at **http://groups. google.com**.

A great site for information on scams can be found at **www.sfwa.org/Beware/Warnings.html**. The site is run by the Science Fiction and Fantasy Writers of America and has a strong bias to the USA. Victoria Strauss runs this section of the site, which is full of valuable tips and information. Despite the US bias, the warnings have a universal relevance.

Here you will find details of agents who charge for reading your work, agents who promise to represent you for an up-front fee and agents who will try anything to get your money before you are published. There are agents who will bill you monthly for 'work' carried out on your behalf once they have you hooked. A reputable agent makes money from representing you and taking a cut of your royalties from your publishers, not directly from you before any of your work is published. Any demands for payment up-front of any kind must be treated with suspicion. Some disreputable agents are linked with unethical or fraudulent vanity or subsidy publishers, receiving fees for referring your work to them. This all applies to bad agents everywhere in the world.

There are 'book doctors' who offer advice that they claim will turn your rejected manuscript into a blockbuster bestseller – for a fee. If publishers are continually rejecting your work you probably have a bigger problem than can be solved by one of these paid editors. Any reputable publisher who believes that your work shows enough promise and is interested in publishing you should have editors to help you if all your work needs is a little polish. Some dubious agents link with these 'book doctors', advising their use before they will 'represent' you –

after having already taken a fee from you, naturally. The agent then receives a kick-back from the 'book doctor', who in turn will recommend other ways for you to spend your money. None of this is meant to say that there are no reputable editors working freelance, of course there are; just as the majority of agents are hard-working, honest individuals. They just need to be chosen with care and with an eye on reputation.

Vanity and subsidy publishers who advertise on the Internet are no different from those you may find in normal press advertisements. There are those that are legitimate publishers and those that are not. These companies may try new ways on the Internet to make it sound other than an almost certain loss of money for you. Many are linked with disreputable agents and 'book doctors'. There are some who will not even print your work as promised, but just take your money – several legal cases are under way in the USA at the moment.

Writing competitions abound on the Internet. Some offer substantial sums as prizes, others offer small sums or no financial incentive at all. You may deem the chance of being published in a well-known ezine a privilege; it adds to your published clips after all. However, there are many competitions to beware of.

Sites that have just started and that need material to fill their pages may hold competitions that offer small cash prizes for one or two of the entrants and use all the submitted material with no further compensation.

Many competitions – and this is true outside the Internet as well – demand an entrance fee. There is a need to be cautious if the prizes are small in relation to the number of probable entrants. A self-financing competition is perhaps acceptable; a profit-making competition is another thing altogether. There is also the possibility of a site that runs an entry-by-fee competition closing down before any prizes are paid. It is possible that sites located on free ISPs are more susceptible to this fraud than sites on subscription ISPs that at least have credit references for their subscribers. A good site with links to various warnings is **http://windpub.org/literary/scams/index.html**.

There are sites that offer you the prospect of being paid from advertising revenue on site. It works this way. You upload an article/e-book and this is held on a page of the promoter's

Website. The page also includes advertisements. For every visitor to the page holding your article you are given some of the money that the advertisers pay. In a letter to the writersweekly.com newsletter (**www.writersweekly.com**) one writer complained that the revenue turned out to be $0.001 per word, or 10 cents per 100 readers. After eight months of her article being on one of these sites she had earned $1.20 and even then could not get the promoter to send her a cheque! While not quite a scam (if they do pay eventually), this is not a way for generating a sensible income from writing.

Read Victoria Strauss's pages at the site mentioned above for more on all of these scams and others. There are also excellent articles on copyright and electronic rights on this site, which are not 100 per cent applicable outside the USA, but which describe in general pitfalls that may be met worldwide. Victoria is a subscriber to **alt.writing.scams** and often gives advice there in response to queries on suspect deals offered by publishers.

In case all of this is making you terrified of using any services offered on the Internet I will repeat that all the above should not give you the impression that there are no good editors, publishers and agents on the Internet – there most certainly are and they outweigh the number of 'bad apples' by a significant factor. The main rule to bear in mind is that you should research before committing yourself to any of them. Use your newsgroups to make enquiries, especially checking past posts to alt.writing.scams in My Deja. Look at the **www.swfa.org** site and use their comprehensive links. Remember that if an offered deal looks too good to be true it probably is. And finally, if money is demanded by anyone other than a reputable editor whom you have searched out personally – not one who has solicited you – think carefully before parting with any cash.

5.6 E-books

There are opportunities for a new kind of book now that text with hyperlinks is available to anyone with a browser. You may remember the adventure or 'dungeons and dragons' books that were wildly popular not so many years ago. These books would have a paragraph or two describing, for instance, the movement of the protagonist (you) through a maze and then offer a choice – if you take the right fork go to section 141; if you take the left fork go to section 196 – where the outcome of your decision would change the flow of the narrative, leading you to, say, treasure with the first choice and a fight to the death with the other. These books are easily re-written for reading on a browser with hyperlinks leading to the relevant sections, so that a mouse click will launch the next section rather than the reader being required to manually search for the right page.

Another use for hyperlinks is in an instruction manual. After a question, the reader is given multi-choice answers, each of which is hyperlinked to a different section of the book. If the questions and answers are well written, an incorrect choice will lead to a section that explains what the reader has misunderstood or not fully grasped in the topic under discussion, while the correct choice will lead the reader to the next stage in the educative process. I remember from my past that, when I looked up the answer to a test question in a textbook and found I had got it wrong, there seemed to be a shadowy figure somewhere giving a smug smile and telling me to read the chapter again. A book that can make a stab at explaining *why* the reader is making mistakes is of far greater value than one that merely says, 'Wrong. Try again.'

The first example is relatively trivial, the second of possible great benefit. Writers, however, are only just exploring the artistic uses of hyperlinks.

Consider the number of computer games that style themselves as 'interactive movies' and imagine what an interactive novel could be like. These novels are being written and are available on the Internet. Hyperlinks lead the reader through an author-constructed maze, offering choices as to where the reader wishes the story line to go. Carefully crafted books of this kind can be read several times over, with different plots, character development and denouements each time.

Here are two articles that further explore the possibilities of hypertext as a writing medium: *Story Shapes for Digital Media* by Katherine Phelps http://www.glasswings.com.au/ GlassWings/modern/shapes and *Authoring as Architecture: Toward a Hyperfiction Poetics* by George Stuart Joyce http:// skyscraper.fortunecity.com/dns/689

Here is an example of the medium. Carl Frederick's online novel *Dark Zoo* is a multi-viewpoint novel where the reader can chose from several characters' points of view. There are six different choices of character, an overall choice of novel and a scrapbook option with photos (**http://www.DARKZOO.net**).

There are books that are written in traditional styles and available on the Internet in several different ways.

Some are completely free. *The Hacker's Diet: How to Lose Weight and Hair through Stress and Poor Nutrition* by John Walker is an example. Try **http://www.fourmilab.ch/hackdiet/www/hackdietf.html** for viewing in a browser or **http://www.fourmilab.ch/hackdiet/hdpdf.zip** for PDF format.

There is another selection of e-books at **http://www.fictionworks.com/esciencefiction.htm**.

Sites may offer the first chapter of a book for free downloading. There will be a fee payable for downloading the remainder of the book. Other sites may offer to post a floppy disk containing a copy of the book; some may offer a choice of e-book or standard print book, with perhaps a free taste for downloading beforehand. Some of these sites are listed in the Appendices. They are often run by e-publishers who will offer royalties of up to 40 per cent to the writers because of their low overheads – but beware of the various scams detailed above. A typical e-book is *Paper Roses* by Celia Collier from DiskUs Publishing (**http://www.diskuspublishing.com/**), which will cost about $6.50 on disk (in the USA) and $3.50 to download from site (anywhere in the world).

Michael Prescott's suspense novel *Stealing Faces* was published exclusively in an electronic format as a RocketEdition six months before its print publication in May 1999.

There have been comments from various sources to the effect that, as they are no more than manuscript clearing houses and are doing no more than acting as agents, e-publishers should charge only the same as agents and authors should take the lion's share of profits. There is another side to this argument which is worth considering. Bonnee Pierson, senior editor/partner at the e-publisher Dreams Unlimited, had this to say in an edition of *Inscriptions*:

> Unknown to most people, we also have investments. Yes, it may not be in an individual book, but I buy disks and packaging materials by the hundreds. An investment that's flexible

and can be used on any book, but an investment nonetheless.

We have to pay for Web space and we've invested literally thousands in programs. Some work and some don't, but we invest that money in the hopes to make a return and, somehow, streamline the process not just for you, but also for ourselves.

We rent Web space. We pay for our Internet time (I spend a minimum five hours a day, seven days a week online). And we invest copious amounts of time into each manuscript. It's not just the reading and the editing. It's the formatting and coding, translating and graphics, time spent in advertising, money spent in print copies for reviews and the shipping costs to get them to the reviewers. And, eventually, ads in magazines like *Romantic Times*.

Then along came the e-reader manufacturers and bookstores. When we set our businesses up, we were determined that the majority of profit from every sale of a book would go back into the author's pocket. After all, it's their dream that's earning the money for my company so they should reap the benefits from it. Keep the prices cheap enough that a buyer would be embarrassed not to try an e-book, but float the largest amount back to the authors who deserve it.

Then the bookstores and e-reader manufacturers come along and wanted their share also. Print publishers don't do direct sales. They're not a distributor or a point of purchase. They're a manufacturer or supplier of a product. They need that middleman, known as the bookseller, in order to make their money. But they also set their retail price knowing that a distributor and bookseller want their piece of the pie. Distributors want an average of 40 to 60 percent off the suggested list price. Booksellers want an average discount of 40 percent. I have two contracts on my desk right now from e-reader manufacturers. One wants 25 percent and the other wants 60 percent.

If we raise our prices to skim back these percentages, we'll be competing in a range with print books. And while I hope to someday compete head-to-head with printed books, we're not at that point yet.

So an e-publisher has costs that you might not have considered. Perhaps they are not so grasping as some would have you believe.

And the publishers in this new market are trying to find their feet as much as the authors are in the new medium.

I remember well the years when the fact that a science fiction book was published under the imprint of Gollancz was all I needed to be assured that I would enjoy it. Seeing the bright yellow dust jacket was an incentive to pick it up. It has been said that e-publishing is today where regular publishing was before the rise of the mega-corporations. Now, as then, it should be possible to choose a book by publisher and editor as well as by author. This may turn out to be the case, but the market needs to be in existence for a little longer before the reputations of the publishers and editors become well known. We can only hope that the huge conglomerates do not gobble up the small e-publishers before we have a chance to find out.

How successful are e-books? Well, in March 2000 Simon and Schuster Online released a 66-page story, *Riding the Bullet*, written by Stephen King on their site **www.simonsays.com**. It was billed as the first initial release by a major international bestseller in this format. When it was put online the demand was so great that the servers overloaded and hardly anyone who tried could download a copy. Problems of overload like this will be sorted out eventually, but it is nice to think that demand could be so high.

In July 2000, King began to produce a novel, *The Plant*, and serialized it chapter by chapter as he wrote it. It was available for download on an honour system – pay $1 for each chapter either before or after downloading. He declared that he would continue writing the book only if 75 per cent of downloads were paid for. The launch began in a blaze of publicity, with press quotes along the lines of: 'Could this spell the end of publishing as we know it?' In November 2000, after five instalments, he stopped writing the book. King says he will write the rest of it at some stage, but has not decided if it will be made available in the same way. Apparently the idea that all Internet material should be free is still widely held, even by King fans.

Sites that carry copies of books for free downloading should beware of copyright. Sites such as Gutenberg (**www.gutenberg.net**), the Oxford Text Archive (**ota.ahds.ac.uk**) and the University of Virginia's Electronic Text Centre (**etext.lib.virginia.edu/english.html**) are very careful about copyright. Anything with ac.uk or edu in the address *should* be as careful, but some of the sites you may come across that are run by enthusiasts might not be. Bear in mind that it could be your book that is being made freely available, or even sold without your knowledge, and think how you would react if that were the case. Act accordingly with other people's work.

There are now hand-held machines (or e-readers) available that will keep e-books on disk and allow you to read them on screen in the same manner as you would use a personal stereo for music. The market for these is so volatile and new that I am not going to describe any one in particular: like any new technology there is shakedown going on that will probably lead to one or two market leaders in the future – and not necessarily one of the current manufacturers.

The principle behind these readers is simple. Download an e-book from the Internet (probably for a fee) and transfer it to your e-book reader or have a reader that is capable of Internet access on its own. The reader will hold more than one book at a time because text files compress so well onto disk. Carry it about like a personal stereo and use it. Watch the share price of battery manufacturers rise.

Several companies now produce e-book readers for the home computer. Microsoft makes a reader, for example, for its own format e-books that can be found at **www.microsoft.com/ reader/default.asp**.

New technology just around the corner is e-paper and e-ink. This involves a flexible thin sheet (the e-paper) containing a dye (the e-ink) that is attached to a spine containing electronics and power source. The dye forms letters in the transparent sheet that can be read – eventually with the quality of printing, it is hoped. When a page is read a button press will erase the words and display a new page. The number of times that write/erase/write cycle will run before the page wears out will be in the thousands, so the lifetime of the page should be reasonably long.

What I find interesting about the attempts to produce hand-held readers is that the printed book is still the best paradigm for the high-tech designs. Is this the best way per se or is it just the best means of making potential users feel comfortable? The technology of the ancient papyrus scroll, for example, still lives on in the column to the right of your word processor or Web browser that gives you the ability to 'scroll' backwards and forwards through text. Time will tell.

If you are interested in writing an e-book here is an article that might be of interest: **www.davidreilly.com/epublishing**.

5.7 Printed books

Sites such as Amazon offer generous discounts on printed books, as do Bertelsmann at **www.bol.com** and others, but remember to factor the postage and packing into your calculations before you swoon over how great a bargain it is.

Incidentally, *all* bargains bought over the Internet should be carefully assessed. Some items might attract customs duties when imported and this could mean that the deal is not so sweet when those costs are factored in; sometimes it may even have been cheaper to buy locally!

Some booksites also offer an out-of-print service that will search for books you may have difficulty finding. You are under no obligation to buy the book (from the larger companies at least) if they find it for you. I recently bought an old copy of a book from Amazon that I had asked them to find over a year before, so long ago that I had forgotten that I had asked for it. When it arrived it was an unread copy priced at about 50 per cent above what would have been asked had it been available on bookshelves. As it had been out of print for 30 years I considered it a bargain and bought it; if I had thought it too expensive I could have declined the invitation to purchase with no fee to pay.

There are other sites that will search a database for books that are out of print and will show a list of booksellers who have copies and their prices, and even offer an online form to complete for ordering the books – an invaluable service when you are looking for that elusive copy of *Letters from a Man o'War* to complete the research on your Hornblower-topping epic. A good worldwide site for this is Advanced Book Exchange, **www.abebooks.com**, another is **www.bookbarn.com** – there are many more. ABE recently found an out-of-print copy of a Lafcardio Hearne book at a reasonable price for my son, who had been looking for it for a long time. It was available at a bookseller in the UK, so postage was cheap. The bookseller was over 300 miles away from our home, so he would never have found it any other way. It was also listed at several booksellers in the USA where the price was slightly cheaper, but the postage would have been more. As with Amazon and bol.com and all the other online stores, do not get carried away by a cheap selling price; it is worth repeating that the additional expenses of postage and packing can spoil your bargain. By the way, the listings often contain rare first editions at enormous prices, so do not be alarmed if the first few prices you see for books you have been seeking are way more than you were intending to spend. Keep looking down the list and you could find an ordinary copy at an ordinary price.

Use your search engine expertise to pin down the sites that really interest you and then use the search facilities within the sites that you locate to get to the book(s) you need.

There is a new technology that is beginning to come in that straddles the fence between publishing and e-publishing and has some implications for writers. This is known as *print-on-demand*. Publishers keep books in digital form on disk and when an order arrives the stored information is sent to a machine that prints and binds just one copy if that is all that is needed. The machine can do this cheaply enough to sell at standard prices too.

Jacobyte Books (www.jacobytebooks.com) is an example of one publisher that offers downloadable digital titles for sale and also print-on-demand. This is great news for the customer. No more booksellers saying plaintively, 'It's been out of print for some time now.' It may not be such good news for writers.

Some of these publishers are allegedly offering contracts to writers that amount to vanity publishing. Several of them have had their names brought up time and again in the alt.writing.scams newsgroup and not to be singled out for praise. If you want to take up a print-on-demand publisher's offer to sell your books for you, check out My Deja for reports and carefully consider the advice given above about subsidy and vanity publishing. If *you* appear to be meeting all or most of the costs it probably is a form of vanity publishing. Incidentally, the above example of a print-on-demand publisher is not a recommendation, merely an example. I know neither one way nor the other how that publisher treats its authors.

Figure 5.4 A typical e-publisher's site

Another problem for writers with print-on-demand is the out-of-print section of any contract they may sign with a publisher. Normally a contract between publisher and author contains a clause that gives all the rights back to the author if the publisher does not reprint the work when requested within a given period, usually in the order of a year or so. The idea is that, if your work is not available in bookshops because the last print run has sold out and your publisher will not make another print run for it, after a set period you have the right to take it to another publisher and get them to print it, or print it yourself, or cannibalize it for other works, or anything you like, because it is now completely your work again. The problem arises with print-on-demand when you try to figure out if your work is out of print. How can it be? An unscrupulous publisher could print one copy each year and tell you that that means it is not out of print. Even an honest publisher could sell one copy a year and have good grounds to say that the out-of-print clause has not been fulfilled, thus keeping the rights out of your hands. There is also a grey area in that if a book is downloaded, does it mean that it has been printed? This is shaky ground again for authors' rights and digital technology, and something that will need to be addressed.

5.8 Rights sales

A new Website was launched in February 1999 by Rightscenter.com, a company that offers the publishing community 'secure global' communication on the Internet, and Bradbury Phillips International, producer of literary rights management software. The site proposes to 'facilitate management and tracking of rights sales online and offline'.

Registration with the site is free and you can register as an author. Your name is placed in a globally accessible directory and samples of your work can be uploaded to the site for general perusal. You can also upload a document to a secure area, send the Rightscenter URL to your target publisher and they can access it. The document will be accessible only to someone you authorize to read it.

The site promises the ability to track the document so that you will know when it has been read, and also the ability to address mail to multiple recipients informing them where the document is. If you are concerned with trying to sell the rights to a long document, perhaps with large attachments, the mailing only has to be done once, to the Rightscenter site. After that you simply need to send the URL to prospective buyers.

It might be worth keeping an eye on this site, as there are some exciting possibilities for selling work here. The site can be found at **http://www.rightscenter.com**.

5.9 Adobe Acrobat

Adobe has produced a piece of software that merits a mention because its documents are completely independent of computer model. As long as you have the reader software that works on your computer you can read an Acrobat file produced by any other type of computer in the world and you are guaranteed to see it in exactly the way it was designed to be seen, with graphics placement, fonts, pagination and so on.

Documents, produced by word processor or desktop publisher, are taken by a program called Acrobat Exchange (new versions are just called Acrobat) and are converted to a format called Portable Document Format (PDF) – the files discussed in Chapter 4. These files, with a .pdf extension, can be stored on Websites or in FTP sites or posted on floppy disk, and when downloaded and viewed with Acrobat Viewer they will look exactly as they did when they were originally made. They can be 'locked' so that they cannot be altered once released, thus ensuring that any PDF file you release will not appear on the Web in an altered form without your permission. The viewer also is designed to make navigating around the book easy. The file creator must be bought and is quite expensive, but the reader is free – a cunning marketing move that has ensured wide acceptance of the format.

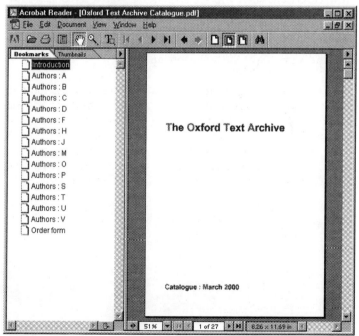

Figure 5.5 The Oxford Text Archive as a PDF file displayed by Acrobat Reader

Adobe now offers a conversion service at **http://createpdf.adobe.com** where you can upload your document and have it sent back to you as a PDF file. Currently, after free registration by entering your e-mail address, you are allowed five document conversions free of charge. Uploaded document files must be less than 100 Mb in size and the conversion server must be able to convert them in 10 minutes. If these parameters are not met your document will not be converted. The site will probably go fully commercial at some stage. There are more details onsite.

The only proviso to the universality of PDF is that there might be problems with A4 (210 × 297 mm), the usual European default size of paper, and US letter size (215.9 × 279.4 mm), the common US default. There are fixes for this if you are producing PDF documents.

Many files are now published on the Web in PDF format so the reader software is becoming an essential add-on to your browser. Often when you see a file on a page offered as a PDF file you will be given the option to download the reader. Otherwise the reader can be downloaded from **www.adobe.com/products/acrobat/main.html** where you will also find some more information on PDF.

Summary

- If you build your own Website be creative and interesting, but don't expect too much from it unless you can offer something really original.

- Consider ezines and online magazines as places where you can sell your work.

- Look for useful guidelines online from print magazines. The number of publications giving guidelines this way will increase, as will ways to submit work online.

- The Internet can be a great place to find collaborators and e-mail is a boon to any collaborative effort.

- Remember that vanity publishing may look different on the Internet. It isn't. Stay clear of it.

- Be wary of any publishing deals that require *you* to pay money. Scams abound.

- The number of e-books can only increase. Look at ways to use this market for your work.

Exercises

1 Find as many online publishers as you can that fit your writing interests. Check their guidelines and try them as an outlet for your work.

2 Look up guidelines for submission to paper publications. See if you can find somewhere that could be a home for your writing and don't neglect any potential foreign markets.

3 If you are interested in writing something for e-publication, think of ways to make it interactive. Check out as many e-books as you can to see how others approach this.

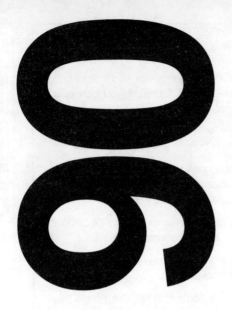

06

serious matters

In this chapter you will learn

- where to find work on the Internet
- about computer security
- how copyright affects the Internet

This chapter brings together three topics related only by the fact that they all deserve serious thought. It looks at the Internet as a source of work, at questions of security – in particular, protecting yourself from viruses – and at the issue of copyright.

Many Websites advertise employment opportunities. Because of the highly computer-centric nature of the Internet, most of the work on offer is in the computer industry, for programmers, IT specialists and so on. There are Websites, however, that offer writing-related work and both the number of sites and the jobs offered are growing steadily.

Here is an article you might like to read that gives advice on how to find jobs online.

♦ *Finding a Writing-Related Job Online* by Greg A. Knollenberg. A freelance writer, Web designer, and computer programmer, Greg is a frequent writer on online writing and publishing, Web design and the Internet. He is the President of Writers Write, Inc. The article also has links to job-related sites. Find it at **http://www.writerswrite.com/journal/dec97/gak3.htm**

6.1 Sites offering work

Journalism

The major work available for writers advertised on the Web is in the field of journalism. A search for 'journalism jobs work UK' on Copernic 2001, a meta-search program, yielded over 400 returns, although that total does include duplicates. The work offered is mainly in what is termed 'new media', i.e. writing news snippets for Websites, ezines or newsletters, but there are some jobs available in the print industry.

Journalists are embracing the new medium with enthusiasm. A great deal of research for articles is being carried out on the Web and this enthusiasm is evidenced by the number of Websites that are devoted to journalism in one way or another. The following sites might be of interest.

www.journalismuk.co.uk
Resources, jobs, magazine and newspaper links.

www.journalism.co.uk
A site where you can advertise your skills for others to find. It is uncertain how effective this approach is, as it relies on a prospective employer trawling for employees. The cost of putting what is a basic CV up on this site is currently £50 for three months' exposure.

www.honk.co.uk/fleetstreet/
Has a selection of resources that might be of use and a forum for professional journalists.

www.newsjobs.net/
Jobs related to journalism, mainly in the USA.

www.asja.org
Home of the American Society of Journalists and Authors.

Editing and writing

The majority of editorial work on offer on the Internet is of a permanent onsite nature. There are some freelance and telecommute positions advertised, however.

The following sites may be of interest:

http://jobs.guardian.co.uk
Job site of *The Guardian* newspaper. There is an archive of jobs from the media section of the paper.

www.recruitmedia.co.uk
Offers both freelance and permanent editorial jobs.

www.tmn.co.uk
A recruitment consultancy with some editorial positions.

http://www.copyeditor.com
Many US copy editing jobs on offer. Jobs are kept on this board for three weeks.

www.sfep.org.uk
The Society of Freelance Editors and Proofreaders is in the process of forming a means of accrediting and registering membership to gain recognition of the professional status of its members.

Newsletters such as *Inscriptions* are an excellent way of finding work. The newsletter editors and contributors do the hard work of trawling the net for publishers who need positions filled. You will find a list of some job-related newsletters in the Appendices.

Just to give an example of what is available in these newsletters, in one recent issue, *Inscriptions* had listings for:

- Senior editor and freelance art editor with a museum magazine
- News reporters needed for health-related newsletters
- Freelance writers to review titles from a catalogue of family videos
- Freelance writers to research and write articles about investment
- Humour columnists for a Web magazine
- Assistant senior editor to monitor a golf-oriented Website
- Freelance writers for 'how-to' articles on running museum shops
- Copy editor for a company publishing several print magazines
- Beauty editor for a print magazine
- Copy editor for a space/science online magazine
- Freelance writers for a travel magazine
- Various editorial positions for a print magazine that also has a Website
- Freelance journalists for a fishery and aquaculture Website with worldwide presence
- Freelance writers for a travel Website concerned with lodgings and hotels
- Copy editor for a teenage print magazine
- Freelance writers for articles on commercial e-commerce
- Assistant editor for a magazine covering plastic surgery
- Manager for a 'teen' Website
- Editor/writer for a print/online communications company
- New products editor for a national trade magazine
- Copy editor/proofreader for a trade magazine

Inscriptions can be found at **www.inscriptionsmagazine.com/** where there is a regularly updated page of job opportunities, most of which are US based, but many of which can be done by telecommuting.

Further lists of jobs can be found at **www.newslink.org/ joblink.html**. AJR (American Journalism Review) job links with a worldwide listing of jobs for writers and journalists. Most of the jobs in this site are US-oriented, but some UK jobs are offered.

It should be emphasized once again that a search on several engines should be the first recourse to find job opportunity sites, especially sites based in your own country.

More sites are listed in the Appendices.

6.2 Security

This section has little to do directly with writing, but addresses some of the questions that beginners have about sensationalized press reports on the Internet and its problems.

PGP

When you send an e-mail to a friend, describing something naughty that you have done, you may think you are talking just to them. You are, in fact, talking to the world – if the world chooses to listen.

Your e-mail does not go directly from your computer to your friend's. It passes, at the minimum, from yours to your ISP's server, from there to a router that works out the best path (often the least busy) your message should take. It then goes through perhaps another one or two machines (sometimes more) before arriving at your friend's ISP. There the mail server stores it and waits for your friend's computer to tap on its window saying, 'Yoo-hoo! I'm ready to receive e-mail!'

The e-mail has now passed through at least three, probably more, computers on its way and as it passes through each computer there is an opportunity for someone to eavesdrop. That someone may be a nasty-minded individual, or the NSA in the USA, or GCHQ in the UK – all nasty-minded, some might think. The services certainly monitor e-mail and do it with programs that seek out keywords and phrases – 'drugs', 'kill the President', 'bomb', 'Semtex' and goodness knows what else.

Do you care? Probably not, if you are like most users. I have not yet personally felt the need to worry over whether or not my e-mail is being read by someone other than the proper recipient. If you do care, because you do not want any prying eyes to read the latest masterpiece that you are sending to your publisher, or your real annual accounts that will soon be on their way to your accountant for him to do something imaginative with, there is something you can do to ensure privacy. You can *encrypt* your files.

The days of lemon-juice ink writing and candle-flame revealing are long gone in the encryption world. Today the USA is desperately trying to curb the use and stop the export of high-security encryption systems, in order to preserve its ability to eavesdrop. Other governments are equally nervous about encryption. Despite this concern, there are programs that you can use legally to keep your mail private and the programs are simple. The best stand-alone program is probably PGP, which stands for Pretty Good Privacy. You may hear terms like 64-bit or 128-bit encryption. All you need to know is that the higher the number, the more secure is the encryption.

I am going to explain some of the details of PGP, without getting technical, so that if you decide to use it you will have confidence in it.

You own two *keys* stored on your computer. These are two long strings of letters and numbers, which are different from each other and are unique. One is your *public key* and one your *private key*. Your public key is made available to anyone who needs it, perhaps by including it in your e-mail signature. The world knows it and it makes no difference to your security as long as you keep your other key – the private one –absolutely private to you.

If two people, whom I shall imaginatively call Amanda and Brian, want to communicate privately, this is how they do it.

Amanda puts Brian's public key into her PGP program and uses it to encrypt her e-mail message to him. Once it is encrypted she cannot turn it back to a readable message again; it is forever gobbledegook as far as she is concerned. She sends it to Brian who decrypts it using his private key, the key that only he knows. He reads it easily and sends a message back to Amanda encrypted using her public key. She in turn uses her private key to read it.

At no stage when in transit can anyone else decrypt and read these messages. They have a secure form of communication. It is pretty good privacy in fact.

E-mails have headers that give information about the source, destination and route of the message. Your software may not show them unless you ask it to, but there is always a header on an e-mail. It does not require an enormous amount of technical know-how to fake a header so that the recipient believes it has come from someone other than the person who really sent it. It could be important for you to know for sure that an e-mail has come from whom you think it has – someone's prank e-mail containing false details purporting to be from another person could lead you to waste time and money or could harm a relationship.

The reason I am explaining this process of encryption in more technical depth than usual is that there is an exciting corollary to the PGP system that requires your confidence if you really need to trust in it. Amanda can use PGP in such a way that when she sends a message to Brian he can know for certain that it could only have come from her and not, say, Catherine. Guaranteed!

> Amanda writes her e-mail. She then encodes it first with *her own private key*, not Brian's public one. This is utterly useless as a secure encryption method. It is weak encryption because the world knows her public key and can use it to easily decode her message. So she now has a weakly encrypted version of her e-mail. However, PGP does not care what it encrypts, it does not have to be plain English, so it will encrypt an already encrypted file just as readily. So Amanda takes her weakly encrypted message and encrypts it again, this time using Brian's public key. She sends it.

> When Brian receives the message from Amanda he can decrypt it straight away by using his private key – remember only he can do this so the message can only be read by him. But he can't yet understand the message; it is still encrypted. He now uses Amanda's public key to decrypt it again and then it is in plain text once more, just as it was when it was first written. He can read it and he can absolutely guarantee that it has come from Amanda, because she is the only one who could have encrypted a message that is broken by her public key. She is the only one with access to her private

key and that is the only key that can encrypt a message that is made readable by using her public one. Neat eh?

PGP is breakable, but only with the use of massive computing power over time. If you have attracted the attention of someone who has access to this power and the time and money to use it on your e-mail, then you are in trouble and probably with the law and the security services. PGP is available for download from **www.pgpi.org**.

It is also available in a commercial version, which is much more user friendly and comes with documentation and bug fixes, from McAfee Retail Software (**www.mcafee-at-home.com**).

Microsoft has a system along these lines built into Internet Explorer. You can find a description of it under 'security certificates' in the Help file. The description given is not particularly good in my view, hence the expansion in this section, which I hope is clearer. Specific help on this can also be found in the *Teach Yourself* series *Quick Fix: Internet Explorer/Outlook Express*.

General security

When you connect your computer to the Internet you are doing more than you might think. You are not just using the Internet, but also becoming a part of it. Connect and your computer is one of millions in the network. This means not only that can you, through your machine, enjoy two-way communication with any other machine that is also connected – whether or not a human is operating it and monitoring its activity – but also that anyone else can communicate with your machine. Someone could be talking to your computer without your knowing.

This might conjure up a picture of doom in your mind.

> If I leave my computer connected while I go and make a cup of coffee, I might come back to find someone has taken it over, taken all my financial details, stolen my file of story ideas, trashed my hard disk, stepped on my tortoise and strangled the cat!

It isn't quite like that, fortunately.

The time to worry about someone hacking into your computer is when you are permanently online and have something to attract a hacker into attacking your computer, such as when you might be running a server hosting a number of others' Websites or running a business that has a Web presence and takes orders and credit card payments. If you are doing this then you will already know about *firewalls* and other defences against hackers. The chances of anyone mounting a serious attack on your computer if you just connect in the way most of us do are just about nil.

Equally, the worry you might have of someone stealing your credit card details when you pay for, say, a book from Bol.com is probably unfounded. There is more chance of the man in the store out in the real world taking your credit card to the back of the shop and copying it, or the carbon copies of your transactions being used to steal from your account. Even so, with the presence of any risk at all the companies that use credit cards over the Internet have set up a protection scheme to guard against theft.

This scheme is know as Secure Socket Layers (SSL). If you are purchasing anything online there should be a message displayed that tells you that SSL is being used for the transaction. Browser software should also show you when this is being used by displaying an icon (of a key, a padlock or something similar) that lets you know when the software is encrypting messages in and out. SSL is built into your browser, so no plug-in program is necessary.

If you need to worry, then worry about your credit card details being stored on the computer that the business owns. That is much more likely to be attacked by hackers than yours, but that is not a problem confined to Internet transactions. Details of your credit cards are flying all over the world down wires each time you use it. Worry has to stop somewhere, but not quite yet. We have to look at viruses first.

Viruses

A virus is a program designed by someone to run on your computer and do things to it that you neither expect nor want and then to replicate itself and 'infect' other computers from yours when it can. (Some of these programs are popularly called viruses when they should really be called Trojan horses or worms, but for our purposes calling them all viruses will be sufficient.)

When a virus program runs it may transfer part of itself to the boot sector of your hard disk. This is the area that contains all the programs that your computer uses when it starts up and once there the virus will run each time you switch your machine on or re-boot it in the event of any problems while using it. It can send itself out to other machines you may connect to, infecting them in turn. It will almost certainly infect any floppy disk you use on your computer, especially system disks that you might use to boot up your machine.

It may call up other programs that will cause mischief – or worse. It could do anything, from just annoying you by displaying a silly message to merely being happy to replicate itself onto other machines when it can, to reformatting your hard disk, trashing all your files in the process. Should you be worried about getting computer viruses just from being connected to the Internet? The answer is no, not if you are careful and take precautions.

It is possible to slip a virus into your computer when you are not looking, but the probability of this happening is remote. The time to be concerned about possible infection is when you are interactively connected, that is when you are receiving e-mail, browsing Web pages or downloading files. Let us look at these in turn.

E-mail and browsing

You cannot be infected by a virus when you are reading e-mail if you read it as a text file. Remember, a virus is a program and needs to run before it can do its stuff. Plain text readers do not run anything, they merely display the text on screen.

If you are reading your e-mail on a Web browser or looking at a page on a site you do not trust (site titles such as 'filez' or 'warez' are particularly untrustworthy) there is a possibility that a piece of code may have been inserted in the HTML page in the form of a Java applet, a script or an Active-X control. You can deal with this by setting security levels on your browser to switch off these functions except when looking at sites you trust. See your browser Help file for setting the security level on your browser.

If you receive an e-mail with an attachment this is really the time to be careful. Dangerous attachments can be in the form of documents or programs.

Documents may have macros embedded in them. These are equivalent to a program in that they run and can perform various activities on your computer. You can set your word processor, spreadsheet or database to ask you if macros should be run or not. If you choose not to run a macro in a downloaded document you will not have all the functions of the document available, but you will still be able to read it. Again, see your Help file for details. Viewer programs are also available as downloads from software company sites or shareware sites and can be used to examine documents safely. They have no built-in functions and only display a document.

Your safest bet is never to open an attached document unless it comes from a source that you trust. Even then you should run a virus detection program on the document before you load it as someone you trust may have been infected without knowing it. The Love Bug, the virus that sent itself to everyone in the recipient's address book before trashing the hard drive, was passed on to millions of people throughout the world in this way. My computer was infected by a similar virus (fortunately

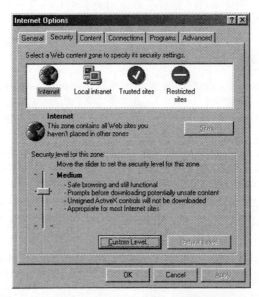

Figure 6.1 Accessing the security settings in Internet Explorer

not a totally malicious one) in March 1999. It was in an e-mail from a friend and had been sent by the virus without his knowledge. I will not run a program attached to an e-mail now without first e-mailing the sender to see if he or she really did send it and then running a virus detection program on it first. A program from *any* unknown source now gets dumped straight away.

Downloading files

Never run a program that you are not sure about, especially from the 'filez' and 'warez' sites mentioned above. Programs normally have suffixes of .exe, .com or .bat, but there are others too. Put *all* downloaded programs through a virus detection program before running them – to be absolutely safe scan *everything* downloaded. You do have a virus detection program don't you? If not, see the Appendices for sites to download from.

The long and short of virus protection is get a virus detection program and use it. Many can be set to run a check on everything that comes to you from the Internet.

Beware of virus hoaxes too. You will undoubtedly receive a message at some stage from someone telling you that a new dangerous virus is loose. You can usually tell it is a hoax from the style. It will contain a LOT OF SHOUTING, will often have several spelling and punctuation mistakes, will be full of dire and ridiculous threats, and will tell you that IBM or AOL or Microsoft is very worried about it. Another big giveaway is that it will tell you to 'pass this on to all your friends'.

Here is a typical hoax virus warning (complete with spelling and punctuation errors) that was actually sent out over the Internet and forwarded to me by a well-meaning friend. It contains most of the pointers to a hoax that these 'warnings' typically contain.

> If you receive an e-mail titiled..JOIN THE CREW/ forPENPALS - DO NOT open it! It will erase EVERYTHING on your hard drive!

> Send this letter out to as many people as you can. This is a new virus and not many people know about it! This information was received this morning by IBM, Please share it with anyone that might access the internet!!

PENPAL appears to be a friendly letter asking you if you are interested in a penpal, but by the time you read this letter it is TOO late. The Trojan horse virus will have already infected the boot sector of your hard drive, destroying all the data present. It is a self-replicating virus, and once the message is read it will AUTOMATICALLY forward itself to anyone who's e-mail address is present in your box!

This virus will destroy your hard drive and holds the potential to DESTROY the hard drive of anyone whose mail is in your box and whose mail is in their box and so on and on! So delete any message titled PENPAL or JOIN THE CREW.

This virus can do major DAMAGE to worldwide networks!

PLEASE PASS THIS ALONG TO ALL YOUR FRIENDS AND PEOPLE IN YOUR MAILBOXES.

AOL HAS SAID THIS IS A VERY DANGEROUS VIRUS AND THERE IS NO REMEDY FOR THIS. FORWARD IT TO ALL YOUR ON-LINE FRIENDS A.S.A.P.!

This is not how virus alerts are sent out. Do not gum up the Internet by passing these hoaxes on. For more information on the subject of these hoaxes and more Internet myths visit **http://kumite.com/myths/home.htm**. And for new virus alerts go to **http://vil.mcafee.com/** or **http://anitviruw.com/vinfo/** – both excellent sites for virus information generally.

6.3 Copyright

Universities are looking at the effectiveness of programs that can search the text of a student's essay and come up with an accurate assessment of whether that particular student wrote it or not. Why should this be necessary?

There are now Websites that contain complete essays on a huge number of topics, produced by writers who are anything from subject experts to other students looking to earn some money. These essays can be downloaded and used as a student's own work. They can be either modified or used 'as-is' if the student is particularly pressed for time. You will, incidentally, not find any addresses for these sites in this book.

The use of the phrase 'can be used' might be misleading. They obviously *are* being used, as the universities' concern makes evident. And why is this happening? Because it is so easy!

When someone downloads a text file of an essay or a book and reproduces it as their own work, the effort involved is minimal. No longer is it a case of painfully transcribing chunks of text by hand from a book, a specimen essay or the work of a friend and laboriously incorporating it into a framework that you have written. With a word processor and a modem all it takes is a few strokes of the keyboard, a wipe of a mouse and a few clicks, and someone else's prose is now embedded into your work. This is readily detectable when long passages are cut and pasted, but not so easy to detect when shorter bits are interspersed with some original work. Hence the academic concern.

The very ease with which text may be lifted seems to lead people to the opinion that what they are doing is not wrong. The above example describes only academic cheating – after all the Website essays are there specifically to be cut and pasted. The next step along the line is plagiarism and abuse of copyright.

The word plagiarism is derived from the Latin *plagiarius*, a kidnapper, *plagium*, kidnapping and the Greek word *plagion* of the same meaning. In use since about the seventeenth century, it is a word that was first recorded in the works of Ben Jonson and, later, Hazlitt. Martial had used it previously in Latin in the context of word theft. The deep feeling of writers for their work is evident in the root of the word – the stealing of a child, an attack on one's offspring, theft of a part of oneself. The Internet is a happy hunting ground for kidnappers.

Looking back at the start of the computing age we can see that the majority of programmers were young and idealistic. The word *hacker* once was not full of opprobrium, but was a compliment, a label for someone who could write good computer code. These hackers had the thought that there should be no copyright on their work and that the brilliant intellectual ideas that they had should be made freely available to others for them to modify and improve. The corporate suits soon moved in and injected commercial realism into programming. Invested money needs protection. Try using some of Microsoft's code in your programming and see how quickly the lawyers fall on you when they find out.

The same ideals were evident at the start of the Internet. Freedom of information was paramount to the academics who ran things. The Net was full of people who cursed commercialism and considered any restrictions at all as censorship. Tim Berners-Lee at the European Council for Nuclear Research who, as far as I know, has not become a millionaire from his work, started the idea of the Web and the HTML mark-up language – an idea that is now generating billions of dollars. You will still come across some of these idealists on the Net. They flame in newsgroups at the slightest hint of advertising. They foam at the mouth over the rampant commercialism that is 'destroying' the community that is the Internet. They constantly declaim that everything on the Net is 'free'. If they believe that they are fighting a battle they can win, I think they are mistaken.

However, despite the rapid changes on the Internet and the avalanche of commercial Websites in recent years, part of the original ethos seems to remain. That is the part that believes that everything on the Internet is public property. It might seem a shame to destroy this last vestige of liberty on the Internet, but it must be done. Not only is everything posted on the Internet *not* public property, it *never was*.

Copyright law is complex and varies from country to country. Bearing in mind that I have no legal qualifications and would urge you to consult better sources if you want information that you can rely on 100 per cent, here is a short breakdown of copyright law as it applies to writers and as I understand it.

UK

Copyright law was modified in 1996 by the grand-sounding document *EC Directive 93/98 Duration of Copyright and Rights in Performances Regulations 1995 (S.I. 1995 No 3297)*. This harmonized copyright laws throughout the European Union.

It is important to understand that only the form in which something is laid out is copyright, not the underlying idea. Plots, artistic ideas and themes cannot be copyrighted. If you feel that an idea of yours for a book or play has been stolen you might be out of luck if you pursue the case, unless you can prove that the form of the plot was stolen. Equally you can apparently pick up ideas from another writer's work in order to weave them into your own – but this does not mean that you can rewrite a Harry Potter book using an identical plot sequence, changing only the character names and altering the words slightly.

Originality is the key to gaining copyright. The work must be the product of the author's skill and labour. All that is required to achieve copyright is to record the work in any appropriate medium. Having it on your hard disk should be good enough. There is no need to publish it, post it to someone or any other cunning wheeze. However, doing any of these extra things does give you some proof should you require it later in any court action. It seems that you do not have to do anything, but if you are paranoid it might help if you do post it to a friend to hold unopened.

Assignment of rights to others is infernally complicated and requires further research on your part if you want to understand it.

It is an infringement of copyright if a substantial part of the original is used and here there is the legal proviso that this is judged by quality and not quantity. Copying is a primary infringement of copyright even if the copying was carried out without the intention of infringement.

Excluded from this is fair dealing, which means that you may use extracts for research, private study, criticism or review. Acknowledgement of the title and author that provided the extracts is necessary and there are limits agreed between the Society of Authors and the Publishers Association as to how much can be quoted under fair dealing. If in doubt ask for permission is a good rule.

Assertion of moral rights (sometimes called integrity or paternity) gives the author various extra rights – the work cannot be treated in a derogatory fashion, for instance.

USA

The USA is slightly different from the UK, but is closer to it than it once was, having now joined the Berne Convention. Foreign authors can now register their copyright in the USA somewhat more easily than they once could. Title 17 – The Copyright Act is the law that applies.

Registration of work with the Copyright Office is now optional for foreign authors, but still apparently a requirement for US authors or authors from non-Berne countries. Registration is still useful for any legal cases that might arise, however. For registration apply to the Copyright Office, pay the appropriate fee and deposit one copy of the work – for more details, visit **www.loc.gov/copyright/reg.htm**.

The owner of copyright in a work published in the USA and containing a notice of copyright must deposit in the Copyright Office two copies of the 'best edition' of the work within three months of publication. Fair use of copyright work is similar to the UK restrictions.

So where does this all leave you as a writer? And what has this to do with the Internet? As a writer you will be concerned that your copyright is not infringed and you should be equally concerned that you do not infringe the work of another. And, despite all the cries that the Internet should be free, copyright is invested by law in electronically reproduced work. In short, everything you see on the Internet, unless accompanied by specific disclaimers and waivers, is safest treated as copyright.

If you create your own Website and use the logo from another site on yours you could be in trouble. The Football Association recently stopped a 16-year-old fan from using the FA logo on his England fanzine Website. Their argument was that, because his site had links to official FA sites, use of their logo gave the impression that the fanzine site was authorized or approved by the FA. Pictures and logos generally are protected by copyright.

Lifting text in great chunks from a Website to use on yours is the same as trying to sell an article to a magazine pretending that the text is your work when you have lifted it from the *Encyclopaedia Britannica*. I cannot see anyone doing that with an article and thinking that they would remain undiscovered, but the number of Websites about that have blatantly stolen text from another is enormous. Somehow Internet users seem to think it does not matter. It does.

The Internet is no different from a printed publication. Rights on the Internet are explicitly covered by electronic rights under copyright law. A September 1999 decision in the USA, 'Tasini v. The New York Times', implies that unless electronic rights are *specifically* signed over to a publisher an article cannot be put on the Web or a CD or anything similar. (See the National Writers Union Website (**http://www.nwu.org**) for further details of this ruling.) This ruling seems to state that, while electronic rights are separate from normal published rights, they are not different. They are rights that are for sale just as much as are First North American Serial Rights or First English Language Volume Rights.

The case of the Northern Light Special Collection mentioned in Chapter 3 is only the beginning of a problem with rights to resell copyright work.

The law is still behind the times in terms of practicality. If I download a Website and store it on my computer I am really breaking the law on copying and duplication. Strangely, it appears that if I then print out the Website on paper I am not breaking the law again. If copyright laws were strictly applied to the Internet, the medium would grind to a halt. Exchange of information would cease. New laws are needed and are coming. Whether or not they will be sensible remains to be seen. Until that time users need to be aware that copyright *does* exist on the Internet and that use of material needs to be careful use. After all, e-mail is quick and text found on a Website that you may wish to use in work you intend to sell will normally be associated with the author's name and e-mail address, so why not use e-mail to get permissions? It is safer, and what is more, will make you feel much more comfortable about using the work of others.

Details for some sites where you can read more on copyright can be found in the Appendices.

Programs and copyright

This might seem a strange place to find a section on computer programs, but they are subject to copyright too. Many of the files you will find on FTP sites, available for downloading, are programs. Many of the programs you will find are shareware. For those who have not come across the concept of shareware here is a quick explanation of various types of program as regards selling concepts.

There are programs known as freeware. The programmer releases these for full public use, free of charge. Some may ask for a donation to charity, some for a postcard to be sent to the programmer; most do not ask for anything, but all are essentially free. These are released as a public service, or perhaps as a demonstration of the programmer's skill in the hope that you will buy some of their other, commercial products, or for other reasons. Do not expect any help outside of built-in documentation or Help files. Sometimes you can get technical help on these freeware programs from the publishing company or the writer, but not often. Many of these programs, such as WS_FTP are extremely popular and you may find newsgroups to be of some help if you run across a problem. Just because they are free does not mean that they are no good. Some of them are excellent – TweakAll for instance (from **http:// www.codeforge.co.uk/home/mainframes.htm**) is a great freeware utility program for setting up parts of Windows 95/ 98/Me that you cannot easily get to otherwise.

Then there is demoware or crippleware. These are full commercial programs that have some essential functions disabled. A graphics program may not allow you to use colour, for instance, or a desktop publishing program may allow you to use every function but not let you save or print your work. Time-limited demonstrations are included with this category. They give you all the functionality of the full-blown commercial program, but will stop working completely after a certain number of uses or after a certain time has elapsed. They may be brought back to life by purchasing a registration number that you type in to 'unlock' the program or may need to be replaced with the full-working version.

Shareware is an excellent concept. Programs produced this way are freely available for download over the Internet. They are usually full versions of the commercial program – although some are limited in their functions, but not to the same extent as demoware – that require registration and a fee if used for longer than about 30 days. They will not stop working after this time, but will often throw up occasional reminders on screen to tell you that you really should pay for the program, or will have delays built into them that slow down the start-up or the speed of some functions. On registering the software – i.e. paying for it, sometimes on a Website – all these annoying reminders will disappear and the program will function normally.

The idea behind shareware is that the would-be purchaser should have a chance to actually use the program thoroughly before committing to purchase in order to be certain that the program does what they want. Although it may run all right without your paying for it, it is not freeware. It is offered for sale this way as a test drive, if you will. If you keep on using it you are morally obligated to buy it. As a writer, you will be understandably concerned with the copyright of your work; shareware programmers are equally concerned about theirs.

Please respect shareware. If you intend to use a program beyond the trial period, then register it. That way more affordable, quality programs will be written as the software writers, who are every bit as hungry as writers like you, will be able to eat.

Good sites for finding these shareware programs are Tucows (**www.tucows.com**), shareware.com (**http://shareware. cnet.com/**) and Jumbo (**www.jumbo.com**). The sites have search facilities to help you find your software by name or category. More sites are given in the Appendices.

6.4 Conclusion

Gains from using the Internet

The revolution that is the Internet is a profound one. It has been compared to the revolution begun by Gutenberg and Caxton – hyperbole certainly, but perhaps not too far from the truth. Whatever the kind of writing you do – fiction, non-fiction, poetry, prose, journalism… – there will come a time in the not-too-distant future when you will not be a fully functional writer if you are not connected to the Internet.

It is still possible to write longhand or to use an old upright typewriter, but writers using word processors can often get their first draft done a little quicker and can certainly manage the re-writes that always seem necessary with a great deal more speed and accuracy. Writing requires skills that no technology can replace, but these skills can be augmented and enhanced.

Writers today who are connected to the Internet are in a similar position to Mark Twain as he hammered out the first-ever typescript of a book. They are using the new technology that will eventually overwhelm the old. It is difficult, if not impossible, to foresee a time when paper books will be completely replaced. It is, however, easy to forecast that more research will soon be carried out over the Internet than in libraries. No one suggests that you tear up your card for the British Library should you be lucky enough to have one – the idea is augmentation, not substitution. The Internet does not and will not completely replace all other forms of research. It will augment them. In Chapter 3 there are powerful tools presented for your use. With a little time and application in learning how to use these tools you will find that research has never been so easy.

Being connected electronically does not mean that you must be disconnected from human contact. The fact that you might be a member of several writer lists and newsgroups on the Internet does not stop you from being a member of your local writers' circle and gaining valuable feedback on your work, as well as networking with other writers face to face. It does mean that the circle of writers with whom you are in contact can be immeasurably wider, with all the advantages that may bring. These advantages could be as varied as fresh perceptions from a fellow writer in Brazil, help with your thriller from an American who knows the mean streets of New York because he lives there, an Australian who can pass you first-hand travel information for the piece on the Great Barrier Reef with which you are struggling.

Who is buying your work? It will not be long before all major publishers, magazines and newspapers have a presence on the Web. That presence can be your open door for access to sell your work. In an ideal world all magazines would have guidelines available for would-be contributors. In the connected world, just around the corner, most will and when the markets change so will the Websites, reflecting new opportunities for selling your skills.

The Internet is a curious organism; it feeds partly on itself and yet it still grows. Many opportunities for writing work on the Net are only advertised on the Net. If you are not connected there is a huge, growing, worldwide market that you are ignoring. Can you afford to ignore it?

Is your writing good enough to satisfy you? Oddly enough, it seems that the better the writer the more dissatisfied he/she is and the more that improvement is sought. The Internet is full of useful articles on writing techniques, most of which cannot be found elsewhere. Find them, get them, read them, and use them! Of course, if you are not connected it is not possible for you to improve your writing that way, is it?

Have you heard the saying that the best way to learn is to teach? A sure way to improve your writing is to 'crit' others' work and – equally important – to read 'crits' written by other writers on the work you have just examined. You may be amazed at how much you can learn from seeing how many different approaches there are to criticizing the same piece of writing. You will certainly find that figuring out why a particular plot development did not work for you as a reader will give you insights on how your own work could be improved. Subject your work to the process and learn. You can do this in local writers' circles as mentioned above, but the volume and variety of critics available on the Internet far exceeds anything you might expect to find locally.

The future of the Internet

Even Mystic Meg would have a hard time forecasting the nature of the Internet in, say, five years from now with any accuracy. The one forecast that can be made with certainty is that it will not be the same as it is today.

With cable networks linking more to the Internet, satellite links becoming affordable and mobile phone networks joining the revolution, one part of Internet activity that will certainly improve is the speed of communication. (See *The Scientific American* site at **http://www.scientificamerican.com/1999/1099issue/1099medin.html** for an interesting article on the Internet via cable.) As new technologies come along, waiting for ages while a large file downloads will be a thing of the past and the increase in speed will enable the easy transfer of files that nobody would dream of trying to send over a telecom link today. How about waiting just a few minutes for the equivalent of the *Encyclopaedia Britannica* to download? What sort of information could be at our fingertips then?

But with this avalanche of information tumbling over us how hard will it be to filter out the bits we need? How much of it can we trust? There needs to be better technology and software to sift through the data and present us with an end product that we can handle with our own internal processing unit we carry in our heads. If we do not develop a means to cope with vast amounts of data it will be useless to us. In fact it will be worse than useless, because it could easily lead us astray. The software and technology will be developed, is my best guess.

As far as writers are concerned, the Internet will only get better. It will become difficult to be successful without being connected. Those who are connected will have an edge. The major magazines and newspapers will all have a significant Web presence and the process of article submission will shift away from paper in the post to documents sent by e-mail. The cycles of query – expression of interest – manuscript submission – acceptance/rejection will run over the Internet rather than in mail vans. Note, however, that there will be no guarantee that the cycle will be that much quicker. Editors will still have slush piles to read through, delaying their response times, but times of messages in transit will be reduced.

The process of publishing should be improved too. On-screen editing and e-mailed queries to authors should speed things up enormously. Transfer of word-processed documents by e-mail and disk between editors, author and printer will mean that delays between manuscript acceptance and publication will be reduced. Cost reductions might even be reflected in increased payments to you.

The growing presence online of libraries and other centres for research will make the writer's task easier. No longer will you need to pore over newspaper clippings for background to an article when newspapers are all archived and accessible on the Internet. You may even subscribe to online newspapers and then effortlessly cut items of interest electronically from their pages to store in your own clippings file on your hard disk. No more manila folders stuffed with yellowing, mixed-up paper clippings!

How international are you now? In a few years there will be few barriers, if any, for a British writer who wants to publish in Australia, America or any other country that wants articles in English. The hassle and expense of getting manuscripts across the world will disappear. The immediacy and cheapness of communication will ensure that wherever the market is, a writer will have easy access to it. Accepting payment for the work might be easier too, as online banking grows.

Translation programs available over the Internet will improve. At present they can take your work or look at a Website for you and translate it into one of several languages, but they cannot do it well. This could radically increase your market as an English writer if you could access foreign markets. Equally, stand by for competition as foreign speakers access your markets. I cannot see software replacing humans in this field for at least my lifetime, but the pace of change is rapid and I could be wrong.

New technology will change the Internet in ways that we cannot imagine at the moment. To give you an example of what is on the horizon, how about this? Imagine that you are at a restaurant and find the service and food appalling or, on the contrary, find that your meal was the best you've ever had. In either case it might be nice to warn/recommend others. Putting a message on a Website would seem to be an inefficient way of telling individuals who are contemplating entering the restaurant about your complaint/delight; the target reader would be very unlikely to read your message before going out to eat and what about the spur-of-the-moment decision that someone may take in the restaurant doorway? How could you get this message targeted properly?

In the USA, mobile phones now have to be fitted with a locater so emergency services can pinpoint the source of a call if required. This locater is usually in the form of a GPS (Global Positioning System) satellite receiver on a chip smaller than a coin. This is a way to achieve what we want. If you leave a message on a special Website and link that message to your exact position (the doorway of the restaurant in our example) anyone with the appropriate mobile phone set-up can receive the message you have sent when they are at, and only at, that same spot. 'Stay away from here! The service stinks!' or 'Do try this place. The food is wonderful!' their phone could whisper in their ears as they stand in front of the establishment.

The restaurant is an admittedly trivial example, but I'm sure you could think of better ones. The point I'm trying to make is that the idea of 'messages in space' is one that is new and could only be implemented as the appropriate technology arrived (Internet, mobile phones, GPS). Not only will the Internet as it stands now be used for things not yet thought of, but when new technology arrives to enhance the Internet even newer ideas will be dreamed up. You can be sure that, as a writer, you will be able to make good use of some of them.

Perhaps I have got it all wrong; perhaps Mystic Meg could do better. Whatever the details, the Internet is here to stay and it will change your life as a writer. Join the international community on the Internet now, or be left behind.

Summary

- The Internet will soon be a very important way of finding writing/editing jobs. The number of jobs offered this way is increasing rapidly.

- Encryption is available if you want your e-mail kept from prying eyes.

- Get a virus detection program. Update it regularly. And USE IT!

- Be very careful about opening attachments to your e-mail. If in doubt DON'T!

- Don't clog up the Internet by passing on hoax virus alerts.

- Be concerned about copyright, both your own and others'.

- Please respect shareware. You will expect others to respect *your* copyright.

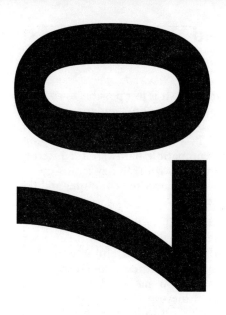

07

how to get on the internet

In this chapter you will learn

- about the basics of connection
- about mail accounts
- about useful software

7.1 What you need

Computer basics

Your first requirement is a computer. It is just possible to connect to the Internet with an old, obsolete, non-standard computer such as a Sinclair Spectrum, but it is not recommended. The standard home computers – PCs and Macs – have an enormous range of software and compatible hardware for Internet connection and are the best to start with. (Sorry if this upsets Archimedes users and others.) The faster the computer and the more memory it has the better.

When you select your ISP they will either recommend software or have their own to give (or sell) as a part of the start-up package. You are strongly advised to take careful note of their software set-up requirements – DNS addresses, ports and other esoteric names and numbers – as you may need them to hand if and when your software goes toes-up. The helpline number and/or e-mail address are also useful to keep near at hand. If you do have problems see 'RTFM' in the glossary before calling the helpline.

Modems and ISDN connections

You need to connect your computer to the phone line before you can communicate so you will need a phone socket somewhere within reach of your computer. A modem is the usual link between computer and phone. This converts the digital output of your computer into an analogue signal that the phone line can carry. This signal is then received by a modem at your ISP that turns it back into a digital signal that their computer can understand. If you think that the translation slows things down you would be right, it does. Not only that, the speed at which an ordinary phone line can carry analogue signals is restricted; speeds at which digital signals can travel are much higher. Because of this there is another way of connecting computers by ISDN (Integrated Services Digital Network). ISDN also requires equipment to be attached to link computer and phone line and is more expensive to use than an ordinary phone.

The best rule of thumb is – faster is better. The lower phone bills when downloading files soon recoup the extra outlay for a fast modem. If you are using the Internet for several hours a day, sending and receiving large files, then ISDN might work out cheaper for you in both time and bills.

Prices change every day, for equipment, ISDN installation fees and phone charges, so there is no way to present hard information that you might use to decide what equipment to buy. When you need to decide you will have to do the sums yourself, based on the charges at the time. It is safe to say that, unless ISDN charges drop considerably in the future, if you are an average writer you will find it more cost effective to use the fastest modem available that is compatible with both your computer and the modems used by your ISP.

There are other, newer, methods of connection. Read the computer press and contact your ISP for details of cable, ADSL and other links. And for UK users there is a Website, **http://www.phonebills.org.uk**, that might help you reduce your phone bills. Visit the site, tell them where you live, how often you use the phone and what kinds of call you make and they will tell you what telecommunications company will give you the best deal. An independent organization, it claims to cover all major UK telecom suppliers.

Incidentally, most modems today also have fax capability, enabling you to communicate with those who are not as technologically up to date as you. Sending electronic documents this way is slightly better than using a real fax machine as the necessary step of scanning a paper into the fax machine degrades its quality a little; the computer avoids this step. The copy you transmit is cleaner. However, there is still the problem of degradation at the receiver's end as the printout capabilities of most fax machines are low quality. If you intend to send printed-paper documents via fax modem you will also need a scanner (which is worth having anyway if you can afford it) to get them into your computer in a transmittable form. This removes the slight improvement, leaving you with something close to a fax-to-fax quality.

When you have an electronic document on your computer that you wish to send to a friend's computer you would be mad to fax it except as a last resort. The print-out from your computer, fax-scan, transmit, receive, print-out, rescan into your friend's computer, run through an optical character recognition program and proofread cycle to return it to its original electronic form would be so time-consuming as to be laughable. You can e-mail it in one step as an attachment. The phone call will be cheaper too.

Phone line problems

The standard phone line will be the normal connection for most of us for a while yet. You will need to find out for yourself if one phone line is enough for you. Using a line for the Internet means that you cannot receive a voice call while your computer is connected. It also means that your connection may be broken if someone else in the house picks up a telephone while you are connected.

If you decide to have a second line installed, then do not be tempted to accept an offer of a 'splitter' that turns your one copper cable into two lines. While this might give acceptable results for voice calls, computers are fussier. Your speed over the Internet will be severely reduced. A genuine second line is necessary unless there have been technology changes since the last time I investigated. Double-check with your telecom supplier if this is offered.

7.2 UK Internet Service Providers

Free services

Once again the constantly changing nature of the Internet has caught me out. When this book was first in outline there were two free ISPs working, with another one about to start. As I write this section there are 20 or so, with more coming. It was intended to compare and individually contrast the free services on offer, but that has now become an unprofitable prospect – this book would need another 100 pages and would lose its focus as a book for writers. Instead, there follows a short description of what you get from these services in general and how they manage to do it.

An ISP that charges you nothing to use it as a connection to the Internet must be too good to be true, correct? The answer is, as usual, neither a straightforward yes nor an incontrovertible no.

Companies that provide free services to you get paid in several ways: through advertising that you either download along with

Web pages or that is permanently displayed by your browser, by a sharing of the phone charges paid by you to your phone company, and in other ways that I do not fully understand. Suffice it to say that all you need to care about is that you only pay phone bills, not a monthly fee to an ISP.

The upside to this is that you get a free service that is no different (depending on whose advertising you read) from that of an ISP that charges you large sums of money every month just for connecting. The downside is that ISPs operate on low margins and the service you get may reflect this. It takes a lot of money to buy server computers and racks of modems; it is expensive to use the backbone services that connect the various elements of the Internet together, and providing technically qualified humans to talk users through problems with programs and Internet connections is not easy or cheap. The service you get might not be as reliable as that from a big fee-charging ISP – you could be plagued with engaged tones when you try to connect, the download rates might be sluggish because of lower equipment standards. Your ISP may suddenly go out of business, leaving you with many people holding your now useless e-mail address or Web page URL and unable to contact you.

It may seem like a good idea to connect to these ISPs for free, try them for a while then abandon them if you are not happy, but things are not quite that simple. Apart from the problems of changing e-mail addresses – as hard, if your circle of Internet friends grows large, as notifying a change of house address can be (see under *E-mail accounts*, p. 166, for a fix for this) – there is the problem of uninstalling the modified standard or proprietary dialler and browser usually provided by the ISP.

Internet connection set-ups can be fragile at the best of times, especially on a PC, and any working set-up you might have with one ISP will probably be completely trashed when you set up another. These Internet connection programs have a habit of walking all over your hard disk in muddy boots when installed, leaving hard-to-erase footprints in important places. When you come to uninstall them do not expect any previously working programs with another ISP to work without the expenditure of considerable time and effort. And if you think that the free ISP's helpline will assist you in sorting out any mess, remember that some of them charge up to £1 per minute for phone help.

None of this should put you off trying free services; you should just be aware that there are pitfalls. If you are confident that you can cope with alterations to your PC, then go ahead. It is rewarding when setting up a service works out, but it can use lots of time that could be more productively used writing or researching your next paying copy.

The next phase in the 'free wars' is a selection of services that offer free phone Internet service for a monthly connection fee. These will involve you in a flurry of calculations before you can be sure that you are getting a service that gives value for money. You will need to guess the number of hours that you will be connected each billing period and calculate the amount you would pay your phone company for normal connection, remembering to factor in the savings from various plans such as BT Friends & Family to which you may subscribe. This amount will then need to be compared to the monthly subscription fee – and do not forget to include VAT.

As I was writing the first edition of this book a new phase was being entered; the ultimate free service with free calls offer, first from AltaVista and with more ISPs following. I wrote that the business plan for this was uncertain and that Internet journalists were shaking their heads and saying that it would not last. Most, if not all, of these services have now ceased. Whatever business model was being used it obviously was not a good one. However, the model of free service provision is not as important as the model of free calls. If this does succeed then Internet use in the UK will expand at a colossal rate.

All of these changes mean that a big shake-up is in the pipeline for services. My crystal ball is no better than yours for descrying the future. All that can be said with certainty is that when the dust has settled there will be fewer ISPs. If you have spent time and maybe money on printing out business cards with your e-mail address, setting up a Website to advertise your services, amassing a list of contacts on the Internet who have your address and configuring your software and computer to work at top speed with your provider, then you will be less than pleased if your ISP is one of those that go under. Unless you choose a big-name long-time provider be cautious about investing too much in setting up any business for which Web and e-mail addresses are essential.

Low-price, pay-per-hour services

Once upon a time there were ISPs that charged low monthly fees and then charged you per hour of online time, either after a set amount of monthly free time had been used or for all of your time online. These are now pretty much defunct as they offered a great deal less than companies like CompuServe and AOL for about the same price. You may find some still in business, but you would need a very good reason for using them in preference to one of the other kinds of ISP mentioned here.

Mid-price, unlimited hours services

Demon Internet was the first of the 'tenner-a-month' services to start Internet connection for £10 +VAT with no hourly charges. Since Demon started, many services have come along to join them: BTInternet, ClaraNet and more. These services provide full connection with Web access, newsgroups, your own Web page space, FTP and almost anything else that the Internet offers. They also offer various extra packages such as fax services and business set-ups, usually for extra money. The helplines are mostly free and available on e-mail as well as phone.

Paying a monthly fee should hopefully give you more reliable connections and this turns out to be the case most of the time. All technology has its problems and the Internet is definitely not an exception, so there are times when connection is not all it should be, but the companies do their best to keep all informed of any problems and spend large sums of money on keeping equipment standards and levels high. Some have their own, ultra-high-speed links to the Internet and so give faster download times.

If you are looking for easy, reliable connection with readily available help for the darker moments, then these ISPs are good and if you join one and find you dislike it for some reason then there is not usually any problem in unsubscribing and trying another service.

High-price content providers

These providers produce a large amount of material that is specific to them. Their sites are designed to be easily navigated and contain news, current affairs information and forums for conversation, information and file downloading. Whereas other ISPs provide just a link to the Internet, these provide a site that is so full of content that they believe many can be satisfied with what is on their network, without needing to link through them to the Internet. Indeed the two main ISPs, AOL and CompuServe – now under combined ownership – were quite late in coming to the Internet proper.

Their basic package is a fixed sum per month plus an hourly charge after using a small number of free hours in a month. Because of this expense these services have been losing customers to the cheaper and free ISPs. As part of a drive to regain their market share of subscribers they are in the process of changing their pricing schemes – the final price packages are yet to be decided at the time of writing – and might have free or cheap phone charges and access charges.

Notwithstanding the caveats, it is worth bearing in mind that these ISPs offer deals on the first month of membership. Most offer 30 days of free access – not forgetting that phone bills still need to be paid unless a free number is part of the 'come-on' package – which gives you a chance to assess their service and see if it meets with your approval. If it does not you can easily cancel your membership and try elsewhere. The caveats about program set-ups apply more than ever here, as the proprietary programs that many of these services use are notoriously difficult to get rid of.

One major advantage of these ISPs is that they have a worldwide presence. If you travel with a laptop, modem and suitable foreign phone connectors you can use the Internet with (usually) local calls from most countries in the world. You will need to do some arithmetic to work out the comparative cost of an ISP account with a monthly fee plus hourly charges against the occasional use of a cyber café or a hotel Internet link. And do remember that access through a hotel switchboard from a phone in your room can attract high extra charges on your room bill – enough to make you faint at checkout if you are paying!

After reading all these descriptions my final suggestion would be to read the computer press, especially those magazines devoted to the Internet, just before you take the plunge and commit yourself to an ISP. Their information and comparisons will be more up to date and there are often pages of useful advice on choosing.

7.3 US Internet Service Providers

The structure of ISPs in the USA is broadly similar to that in the UK as described above, one difference being that, since the Internet has been a consumer product for longer in the USA than the UK, the shake-up of ISPs and pricing structures is probably about a year or so ahead, according to a knowledgeable friend in California. Free ISPs abound and offer basic services. Pay-per-month ISPs usually offer more facilities, such as Website hosting. AOL and CompuServe are big movers and shakers – AOL stands for America On Line after all. The difference in the pricing of telecom services is what makes a big difference between the USA and the UK.

Internet users in the UK are under the impression that phone calls in the USA are free. This is a myth; they are not. However, they can be cheaper than in the UK and just happen to be organized in such a way as to often make Internet use much cheaper.

In a normal deal with a telecom company there are two different account structures, one for business and one for personal or residential use. Business is more expensive and generally does not give any free 'message units'. Residential use is the deal to get when you are going to connect to the Internet. Bear in mind that, since deregulation and the ensuing enormous increase in the numbers of competing phone companies, pricing structures vary wildly from state to state, and even from location to location within a state.

A typical telephone utility company will offer either a deal that gives cheap monthly payments with 'per minute' charges increasing with distance bands, or a deal that has a slightly higher monthly payment with unlimited free 'local' calls and charges on the longer distance calls. The payments for the first deal might be around $5 to $8 per month and for the second around $15 to $20 per month. (This does not include the numerous local taxes, etc. that will push prices up a little.)

The 'local' calls are limited geographically by distance from residence to local exchange, but a 15-mile radius from home is a good guide. This means that if you live in the centre of Los Angeles you will be within reach of several exchanges inside that distance. Living in the middle of the desert is going to restrict you a bit more!

Let us just look at my friend's ISP and telephone accounts as an example of what can be available for you in the USA.

After using a combination of free ISPs and a $5 per month e-mail provider with Web browsing time limited to two hours a day, he has changed to a service giving full Internet access, a hosted Website and unlimited online time for $12.50 per month. This is in the low range of pricing, some ISPs charging up to $20. His phone company charges him $25 per month for unlimited 'local' calls (this time including taxes). Since he lives in LA he is within the 'local' range of several exchanges where his ISP has a number. Most large, free ISPs have at least one number in his local calling area so there are others available should he choose to change for some reason. He runs several Websites free and only pays a $35 per year charge for registering his .com and .org addresses. Therefore he has unlimited access to the Internet at any and all times for a fixed price of $37.50 per month (approximately £24).

He is currently looking at an ISP called Free DSL Services. They are offering a Digital Subscriber Line giving free access to a high-speed (50 times an analogue modem rate) full-time 24-hour/7-day Internet connection. This normally costs around $50 per month, so if they can offer a local number he would have permanent online connection for free (excluding the one-off purchase of the special modem needed). Free DSL Services can be reached at **http://www.free-dsl-services.com/**.

And here in the UK, we have BT. Ah well, things may change.

7.4 E-mail accounts

Microsoft offers free e-mail accounts with HotMail and several other companies do the same. The major advantage of using this service is that you do not need to connect to your own ISP in order to get mail. With an Internet connection on a computer, such as at a cyber café, library or hotel business suite, and a program such as Microsoft Internet Explorer or similar on the computer, you have all you need. Ask for your mail and it shall be delivered.

One disadvantage of this approach at a cyber café is that your mail is not stored on a disk for you to work on it offline. Reading and replying must be done while connected, which means the time you are paying for gets eaten up unproductively. Another disadvantage in using this for your only e-mail resource is that you will find it difficult to get a meaningful e-mail address – those using CompuServe and AOL have this disadvantage too. So many people are connected through these companies that names are now linked with numbers, so if I wanted to be known as **john@hotmail** I would wind up with something along the lines of **john3876987@hotmail**, a truly memorable address I am sure you will agree and one you would be proud to put on your business card. Not. Hence there is a desperate search when signing up to find a name variation that few others have used. My son picked an obscure Japanese film title for his HotMail nickname and still found that 68 people had chosen it before him.

A service that has been designed specifically for those who change ISPs frequently or move from one corporate or educational site to another is *e-mail forwarding*. For a fee a company will give you a virtual e-mail address at that company. This address is the one you give to people who might want to mail you. The forwarding company holds your real e-mail address so that when mail arrives it will be sent on to you. When you change your ISP or leave college or join another employer, all you need to do is to contact the forwarding company online and alter your forwarding address. In effect the world only ever sees one e-mail address for you, never knowing that you might have changed your real address several times.

Permanent Website redirection is also offered by some of these companies. Here you give out one URL to the world and, no matter how many times you shift your Website from one domain to another, keying in the original URL will always get a browser to your site.

There are several of these companies in the UK and the USA (see **www.pobox.com** for one example). A search on 'e-mail AND forwarding' should find many companies to compare and choose from if you feel you need this service. Costs do vary so have a good look before you jump into a deal. It is certainly a fix for the problem mentioned earlier regarding changes of address.

7.5 Software

There are books that are written specifically to guide you around the Internet software and connection minefield. The following section is meant as a rough and ready guide only. For fuller details I would suggest you try *Teach Yourself The Internet* by Mac Bride (Hodder & Stoughton in the UK or NTC Publishing Group in the USA). For guidance with specific software packages and operating systems, the *Dummies* series (IDG Books Worldwide Inc.) is good for basics, although you will outgrow it quickly, and both Sybex Inc. and Ziff-Davis Press produce excellent advanced guides. These do tend to be expensive, especially in the UK where US dollar to pound price conversions are often $1 = £1 when the books have anything to do with computers.

Basics

Microsoft Windows 95/98/ME has software included that will deal with your dial-up side of connection. The Help files will guide you through the process of setting it up. Those who own Macs will find an easy set-up routine with the provided Internet Setup Assistant. With a Web browser and an ISP you have enough to start surfing.

The browser supplied with the Windows software is now Internet Explorer (IE, current version 6). If you have an earlier version than IE6 it is worth upgrading it. IE6 is available in many places on the Internet, but Microsoft's Website is a good place to find the most recent version (**www.microsoft.com**). It is also on many magazines' free cover CDs (much quicker than downloading from the Internet) and will come with most software that an ISP provides. It is provided as free software.

If you want to try a different browser then Netscape Navigator is as good as Internet Explorer. It can be found on the Netscape site (**www.netscape.com**) and again on free CDs. It is also free of charge.

Getting Microsoft Outlook Express or Netscape Messenger for dealing with e-mail gives you the basics. These are available for free on the above sites and once more on free CDs. Other dedicated mail programs are available.

The free iTools software (**http://www.apple.com/**) offers a lot for the Mac user with OS9.

There are program suites that will cover all of your basic Internet needs. One of these is Turnpike. I use this program because I started years ago with it as a DOS program and have watched it grow into a mature Windows-based program. If you join the ISP Demon in the UK the software is provided on CD with your joining package. It's darn good. If you want to try it you can read about it and download it from the following site, but be warned, being more than 10 Mb it's a hefty download (**www.demon.net/products/turnpike/**).

One program that you will certainly need is WinZip. This is a shareware program that takes a file and compresses it to a fraction of its normal size. This zipped file will transfer much faster over the Internet, considerably reducing time online. Many of the files you will find are zipped and you can recognize them by the suffix .zip after the name. When you run WinZip on a zipped file it is returned to the original size, no information having been lost in the process. Plain text and word-processed documents lend themselves well to being zipped; compression factors are high. Graphics files that are already heavily compressed, such as GIFs or JPEGs, can actually grow in size when zipped. WinZip can be obtained through **www.winzip.com**.

Plug-ins

There are additional programs obtainable (for free) that allow you to see and hear clips that designers have put on their Website, view some types of page or carry out a task that your basic software cannot do at all or as well. These are known as plug-ins and work with your other Internet software. Those shown below will get you started, but there are more. Normally if a site requires you to have a plug-in for viewing part of it there will be a link to where the plug-in can be downloaded. Do remember the virus dangers when downloading 'special viewers' from sites belonging to individuals when you are required to download direct from the site you are on rather than link to another, well-known site (see Chapter 6). Many plug-ins are given away on free CDs.

Adobe Acrobat Reader
Reads pages in the PDF format.
www.adobe.com/products/acrobat/

QuickTime
Displays movie clips and animation.
www.apple.com/quicktime

RealPlayer
Plays audio and video clips.
www.real.com

Shockwave/Flash
Viewing movie clips and animation with some interactivity.
www.macromedia.com/software/

Additional software

Copernic
Meta-search program. The free, trial version is limited in use compared with the full version, but still good.
www.copernic.com/

mIRC
Free Internet Relay Chat software.
www.mirc.co.uk or www.mirc.com

Web Ferret
Free meta-search program. Other excellent (commercial) programs on site.
www.zdnet.com/ferret/index.html

WS_FTP Pro
Full commercial version of the file transfer program. Available for a 30-day evaluation.
www.ipswitch.com/Products/iws_ftp/index.html

WS_FTP LE
Free version of the above program. Fewer features, but still good.
www.gabn.net/Junodj/ftpdesc.htm

General software download sites

DaveCentral
Enormous Windows and Linux archive.
http://www.davecentral.com/

Download.com
From CNET, hundreds of PC and Mac files.
http://download.cnet.com/

Jumbo
Over 300,000 files.
www.jumbo.com

Pass The Shareware
Plenty of shareware and freeware here.
www.passtheshareware.com

Shareware.com
Again from CNET, this is a huge shareware site.
http://shareware.cnet.com/

Tucows
This site rates software by a score out of five. Both PC and Mac.
www.tucows.com

Writing-specific software

Sandbagger's Site
There are some good articles on this site, but this is the home of Sandbagger's Automated Manuscript Management Software (SAMM). It works with DOS or Windows and does a good job of tracking where your work has gone, sometimes a complicated task. I use it and like it.
http://www.sandbaggers.8m.com/

Software for Writers
A site with links to sources of writing software.
http://mockingbird.creighton.edu/NCW/software.htm

Writers' Software Advices Store
Directory of software categorized by specific writer's needs.
http://www.software-for-writers.com/

taking it further

For those of you who really are beginners with computers and/or the Internet the learning curve is very steep when you start and it is very easy to be put off by the apparent obstacles that seem to stand at every point of the learning period. The technology can be intimidating, the jargon used can be quite obscure and parts of some programs (especially the Help files!) appear to be written by little green men from Mars. However, there are plenty of 'hands-on' courses available under various adult education schemes and if you do run across problems I would urge you to try one of them instead of just giving up. It won't be long before you will look back at tasks that once appeared insuperable (and even totally incomprehensible) and wonder to yourself what the problem was.

In the USA the Office of Vocational and Adult Education (OVAE) gives assistance on where to find such courses. You can find more information at **http://www.ed.gov/offices/OVAE/**.

In the UK, your local library or Citizens' Advice Bureau will be able to point you in the right direction for courses near you. There may even be information on a Website run by your local town or county.

Despite the increasing spread of the Internet, paper publication is doing better than ever – good news to those of us who try to make some money from writing. There are still sources of aid for you as a writer that are best read or only published as books.

It's pretty pointless to attempt to recommend books on how to get to grips with any specific program you might be using; the list of books would be endless and might not even cover your favourite program. The standard of computer books varies wildly and, in general, it is fair to say that you should go for the books you feel comfortable with after giving them a short browse. You could even ask around your new Internet writing communities for advice on which books have satisfied others!

One problem that does occur is that you will rapidly gain expertise when you use a program – Windows, Mac OS, browser, word processor, Website designer or whatever. This means that any book you buy when you are a complete beginner will probably soon be of less use to you than you imagined – the book that you are reading now is not one of them, naturally! Take care, then, to ensure that your purchase has some lasting value. You will certainly need the basics explained, but you will eventually (and sooner than you might think) need to have some more detailed explanations of the cleverer parts of your program. Perhaps the best way might be to buy a cheap basic book to begin with and be prepared to buy something more complicated (and unfortunately more expensive) later. Some of the basic books available are surprisingly expensive anyway and really don't seem to be very good value for money. In the UK, of course, we are back to the apparent dollar per pound currency conversion rate for American goods. Another approach might be to purchase an 'intermediate' book that will last you a little longer than a basic book, while still covering enough of the basics to be of value at the start of your journey.

You can't beat hands-on experience, but some general books on the Internet will help to gain a better idea of what is out there (and perhaps help to curb any initial over-optimistic expectations). *Teach Yourself The Internet* by Mac Bride (Hodder & Stoughton Educational) is a good starter. In the same series, *Teach Yourself the Internet for Students* by Chris Wright covers a lot of sources for information that a writer will find useful.

If you are interested in the beginnings of the Internet I recommend *Where Wizards Stay Up Late* by Katie Hafner and Matthew Lyon (Touchstone imprint of Simon & Schuster, New York), a well written, humorous and fascinating look at the origins and early years. It should give you a good feel for what the Internet actually *is* rather than what the media hype makes it out to be. *Cyberpunk: Outlaws and Hackers on the Computer Frontier* by Katie Hafner and John Markoff (Touchstone, 1991) is another book for those interested in what happens 'behind' the Internet. An account of the hacking subculture, it gives the inside story of several hacking groups, their techniques and the motivations behind their crimes. It also gives an insight into what the Internet actually is.

For your writing generally rather than the Internet specifically, *The Writer's Handbook* (Macmillan, London), published annually, is invaluable for UK writers, and for US writers the annual *Writer's Market* (Writer's Digest Books, Cincinnati, Ohio) is equally invaluable. Both contain a wealth of useful website addresses and both have been mentioned in previous chapters. Also, don't think that just because you live in the UK you can't sell your work to the USA, and vice versa; you can get hold of both books in either country.

Research for Writers by Ann Hoffmann (A & C Black, London) comes highly recommended as a book that should be on every writer's shelf. Although direct mention of the Internet is quite limited, the basics of research are covered in depth and the rules laid down for good, accurate research apply equally to Internet use. If you're ever stuck for a research source, look in this book and you'll find several different directions to run in. With practice you may also devise the means to use the Internet to access sources very similar to those to which Ann Hoffmann refers; her mentioned sources may even be on the Internet by the time you look. Equally, don't forget what I've probably bored you with already; the Internet *augments* research and you shouldn't just give up if you can't find the answer to your particular problem online. Try the Internet first – especially sites like **www.libraryspot.com** that can lead you to many other sites – but be prepared for some library and archive visits in person if necessary.

When it comes to research please also don't forget the CD ROMs (and DVDs too) mentioned in Chapter 4. The purchase of a good reference such as *Encyclopaedia Britannica* on CD will repay its price many times over in saved research time and costs. It may be drier and less 'glitzy' than Encarta, but it contains a lot more raw information that will be of use to you as a writer.

Finally, and with no real connection to the Internet, for those writers who are interested in the editing side of the profession (and really we all should be) *Copy-Editing* by Judith Butcher (Cambridge University Press) is a marvellous book. The author, once head of the copy-editing department of CUP, is knowledgeable and writes with refreshing clarity. This should help writers to produce better manuscripts – thus improving the chances of being read seriously on submission – and will also help them understand why their work has been edited the way it has been when returned by the publishers. As someone who wears a copy-editor's hat as often as he wears a writer's I can tell you that my copy is very well thumbed.

There may come a time when you will want to create your own Website to display your writing skills. You can, if you wish, learn to write pages in HTML (HyperText Markup Language) or even use the new, and far more powerful, XML (eXtensible Markup Language). However, there are programs that will help you to create a good-looking site without this learning process. You pay, though, for the time and effort saved in not learning a programming language with the expense of the program purchase and the time spent becoming familiar with its use. There are many Web design packages for sale, ranging from cheap to extremely expensive, with the cheapest not necessarily being the worst and the most expensive not automatically the best. Read the computer press, either on paper or through their Websites, for reviews of the programs before you splash out your cash. As an example of what one of these programs can do, the Website that goes with this book, **www.valley. demon.co.uk**, was created using Microsoft Front Page 2000, which gives the flexibility to design a site that is individual rather than one that fits only a restricted number of pre-designed templates. It's one of the most popular and fits in the mid-range for price. Its latest incarnation at the time of writing is Front Page 2002; which raises another point.

If you are earning money from your writing, you know already how difficult it is to sell your work and how little it seems that you get in return for it. If you aren't earning money from writing (yet!) your position is even worse. Resist the temptation to keep up with the latest in computer programs and you'll save a large percentage of your hard-earned money. There is little reason to buy the newest word processor, for example, if the one you have at the moment is really all you need. If it does the job, my advice is to keep it; you can usually find work-arounds to overcome minor problems – bearing in mind the collaborative problems mentioned in section 5.4. As an example of what can be done with 'old' technology, the first edition of this book was made with files in MS Word 2.0 format typeset in Pagemaker 5, both programs being several years old and many versions behind the current ones. When you do feel that your ancient program needs updating, you don't necessarily even need to buy the latest version. The auction Website eBay (**www.ebay.com**), among others, often has versions of programs for sale that are older than the current, but perhaps newer than yours. There are other sources for these programs on the Internet and there are also some retailers (high street and Internet) with good deals on 'older' versions and even street markets (although there you should beware of pirated editions – if you want to get a virus on your computer a pirate disk is a good way of doing it).

With the Internet developing and changing, and new resources coming online all the time you may find it difficult to keep up. Many newspapers have sections on the Internet, there are numerous magazines on sale devoted to it and you should try to note down any interesting sites mentioned that you might want to use. Naturally, the other Internet users you communicate with will be sources of new developments. As I write this there are flurries of enthusiastic press releases in the UK for the Public Record Office's recent release of the 1901 Census online (**www.census.pro.gov.uk/**). Millions of simultaneous attempts to access the site have led to its crashing, but this will certainly be sorted out eventually. This resource, along with other census results to be released in future and the many census and immigration records already online in the USA, could be invaluable to those writers engaged in biographies or searching for background information on locations. There are valuable resources being made newly available to you all the time. It's up to you to find them. If you use the ideas offered in this book, I hope it will make the finding easier for you. I'm sure you'll come up with ideas of your own after a short time as an Internet user. If you do, why not share them?

glossary

If you meet a term that you do not understand and that is not explained here, or cannot understand my explanation (hopefully not the case!) a splendid site that gives full A to Z listings of Internet and computing terms can be found at **www.netlingo.com**. Another explaining terms, background technology and a lot more besides is at **www.whatis.com**.

General computer terms

Client A program or computer that demands information from another program or computer. See **server**.

Server A program or computer that acts as a source of information or resources for other **client** programs or computers. When you access a **Website**, your computer (client) talks to the computer (server) holding the **Web pages**.

Unix (*you-nicks*) An operating system used by many of the major (or backbone) Internet servers.

Internet computer terms

Active-X A programming language from Microsoft that sits on your computer and runs programs that automatically download with **Web pages**. This enables you to interact with the page in various ways that make reading the page more interesting than just reading text and looking at static pictures.

applet A small **Java** program that sits on a **Web page**.

attachment A file included with an **e-mail** message.

BBS Bulletin Board System. An old term, still sometimes used, that describes the system that allows many users to send messages to a common address where they can be read without all the users having to be connected simultaneously.

bookmark A way that the Netscape **browser** memorizes a **Web** address. Microsoft calls bookmarks favourites. Bookmark has become almost a generic term.

bounce Mail which fails to find its addressee is bounced or returned to the sender. Sometimes used to describe mail sent to a mailing list address that bounces onward to a list of subscribers.

browser A program such as Microsoft Internet Explorer or Netscape Navigator, that enables you to connect to the Web section of the Internet.

bulletin board A collection of files and messages on a computer available for a member to **log in** to access using **TELNET** or other similar program. Also the Microsoft name for what CompuServe calls forums.

channel A named area on **IRC** where specific topics are being discussed.

chat area Part of a **Website** that can be visited and where you can 'talk' to other members visiting the site at the same time as you.

cookie A small file that a **Website** stores on your hard disk and on its own in order for the site to know various things about you when you re-visit. If you do not want to let sites place files with unknown information on your disk your browser can be set to not accept cookies. Warnings about some sites being inaccessible or not working properly if the cookie function is turned off can be safely ignored. If a site refuses to work you can always just turn the function on again for that site.

domain The part of an Internet address that is the name of a computer or a network. Found to the right of the @ sign in an **e-mail** address and to the right of www in a **Web** address. In **bgates@microsoft.com**, **bgates** is the addressee and **microsoft.com** is the domain name. In **www.microsoft.com/public/** the domain name is again **microsoft.com**.

DNS lookup Domain Naming System lookup. The Internet

does not understand the names contained in a **URL** and conducts a DNS lookup in order to convert names to numbers. While an address like 255.125.46.67 is easily recognizable to the Internet, it is a lot harder for a human to remember than microsoft.com. If a **server** you are trying to connect to is off the **Web** for some reason, or you have entered an address for a domain that does not exist, you may see a 'DNS lookup failure' report.

download Receiving data from a **server** to your **client** computer.

DSL Digital Subscriber Line. A way of using the normal copper cables that your telephone line operates on for sending digital rather than analogue signals. Speeds of data transfer are very much faster – up to 50 times faster. A special modem is required.

e-mail Text and other data sent from one computer system to one or more remote systems.

favourites Microsoft's name for **bookmarks**.

FTP (*eff-tee-pee*) File Transfer Protocol. The language used to transfer files of information or programs across the Internet.

gopher An older system of searching the Internet for resources. Menus of resources are displayed similar to a library index. Still in use in the academic world, but easier systems are now available.

home page The start page of a **Website**. Loaded by default if no other page is asked for, it will contain **links** to other parts of the same site, much as an index in a book.

host A computer or computers on a network that offers services such as database facilities or **Websites**.

HTML HyperText Markup Language. The language used to write **Web pages** so that **browsers** know how to display them. Pages held on a site will usually have the suffix .htm or .html.

http HyperText Transfer Protocol. The language used to transfer **HTML** files (**Web pages**) across the Internet.

hyperlink See **link**.

ICQ 'I Seek You'. A program that enables two people to know when the other is online and allows them to chat.

IRC Internet Relay Chat. A system that enables you to 'converse' with another person in real time over the Internet.

ISDN Integrated Services Digital Network. Data is transferred over the normal phone lines as a digital, rather than analogue, signal. Speeds are much higher than with analogue modem connections, but prices are higher as well.

ISP Internet Service Provider. The company that you connect to over the phone lines that in turn connects you to the Internet.

Java (*Jar-vah*) A programming language that was devised so that code written in it would be compatible with all types of computer, PC, Mac etc., without having to be rewritten for each type. It enables **Web** designers to include multi-media effects and interactivity on a **Web page**.

Kb/s Kilobits per second. A measure of modem speed. Higher is better!

link or **hyperlink** A line of text or a graphic that, when clicked with a mouse, takes you directly to another part of the document you are reading or to another site or page on the **Web**. Links are usually highlighted in some way, blue underlined text being common.

log in Some sites, especially those that are only available for a fee, require you to enter your name and a password before accessing the site. This is known as logging in, logging on or signing on.

mailing list An **e-mail** address that corresponds to a list of subscribers. Any mail to this address is redirected to all others on the list.

mailreader Software that lets you read **e-mail**. The popular **browsers** have this built in.

MHz Megahertz. The speed of your computer processor. This has no direct effect on the speed of your Internet connection, but higher speeds will improve the speed of your display.

mirror-site Speed of downloading is improved by both reducing traffic on a site and by using a site that is geographically close. Many major sites – especially FTP sites, the Gutenberg sites being a good example – are duplicated around the world. These extra sites mirror the files at the first, thus giving you a choice of connections. This both decreases traffic on any one site and enables you to select a closer site than the original. Mirror sites are continuously updated to synchronize files with the original site.

news server A computer that holds **newsgroup** messages.

newsgroup A collection of messages held under one name by a **news server** and available for the public to **download** from and **upload** to. A group may be thought of as a topic discussion area.

newsletter A letter sent by **e-mail** at intervals to subscribers. Available on many topics, some newsletters are free whilst others require a fee.

newsreader Software that lets you read messages on **newsgroups**. Some popular **browsers** have this built in.

offline Not connected to the Internet. **Mailreaders** have an offline reading facility to enable you to read at leisure without racking up large phone bills.

online Connected to the Internet. The phone bills tick away.

page A **Web** document, usually with the file suffix .htm or .html. Held on a computer and **downloaded** by your **browser** for you to view.

plug-ins Small programs that your **browser** needs to show files of different formats.

PoP Point of Presence. Your modem has to talk to one of many modems located at your *ISP*'s physical site. The modem you talk to is the PoP. Most ISPs provide local call facilities for wherever you are in the country and when you connect using this facility you are said to be connected to a Virtual PoP.

POP3 Post Office Protocol 3. A fairly recent version of **e-mail** receipt. POP3 is a **client/server** protocol where e-mail is received and held by your server. When you connect to your server your mail will be waiting for you to **download**.

portal A site that hopes to act as your access point to the Internet, the page that you always load first in any Internet session. It will usually provide **e-mail** facilities, **chat** areas and other 'value-added' extras and will often be capable of being personalized to show regularly updated information that you request to be displayed.

postmaster As in **postmaster@wherever.co.uk**. **E-mail** sent to a postmaster address should get to the person who runs the mail side of the **domain**. It does not always work.

protocol The language that computers use to communicate with each other on the Internet.

robot In Internet terms, a program that runs a mailing list or collects information about **Websites** for an index without any human intervention. See **spider**.

script A series of instructions that run like a program.

search engine A **Website** that has search facilities enabling you to search for a specific topic on the **Web**.

site A location, usually on one **server**, where a collection of **Web pages** or files for **FTP** are kept. The address of the site is expressed as a **URL**.

SMTP Simple Mail Transfer Protocol. An older system of **e-mail** transfer, gradually being replaced by **POP3**.

spider Sometimes called a **Webcrawler** or **robot**; this is a program that visits **Websites** to extract information for a **search engine**.

TCP/IP Transmission Control Protocol/Internet Protocol. The common language that enables many different types of computer with different operating systems to communicate.

TELNET A protocol for running another computer over the Internet from your keyboard. Character-based only and working on Unix commands – you cannot run anything like Windows on the other machine. Used with some **bulletin boards** and some library catalogues.

thread A collection of posts that are connected in some way by their content – usually replies to an original post and replies to the replies.

upload Sending data from your **client** computer to a **server**.

URL Universal Resource Locator. The address of a **site** on the **Web**.

USENET A network sharing public messages – now more or less synonymous with **newsgroups**.

virtual hosting If your **ISP** holds your **Website** for you it is acting as a virtual host. Your Website is accessible to others without your own computer at home being permanently connected to the Internet.

Web Short for World Wide Web. The area of the Internet that can be reached by a protocol such as **http** that can be understood by a **Web browser**.

Web browser See **browser**.

Web page See **page**.

Web ring A way of interlinking **Websites** that are related by subject matter so that you can easily visit each site in turn. If you continue visiting sites in the ring you will eventually return to your starting site.

Webcrawler See **spider**.

Website See **site**.

whois A **Unix** command used with whois **servers**. The servers contain lists of **e-mail** addresses; whois jralph shows information about jralph if the server has any. Far from being 100 per cent reliable and now mostly used by academics.

winsock WINdows SOCKet. A PC program that enables the Windows computer operating system to translate the **protocol** used by Internet programs to communicate across the **Web**.

www World Wide Web. See **Web**.

XML eXtensible Markup Language. An extension of **HTML** with far greater capability.

Internet slang terms

bandwidth The amount of data that can be transmitted across the Internet from source to you in a given amount of time. The larger the bandwidth, the faster data is transferred. Sending **e-mail** replies to someone containing all the text that was sent to you originally along with your reply is said to reduce or waste bandwidth.

cross-posting Sending the same message to several newsgroups simultaneously. A lot of **spam** is cross-posted.

delurking After being an inactive member of a **newsgroup** or **mailing list**, the act of posting your first message is delurking.

emoticon See **smiley**.

FAQ Frequently Asked Questions. A list of queries that has been most often raised in a **newsgroup**. Posted to some groups at intervals in order to reduce the number of times that the same questions are asked over again.

flame A critical, often highly outspoken and rude attack on someone for something that has been posted by them.

flame war A series of **flames** between (at least) two people with (at least) two different viewpoints over a posted message.

flamebait A **post** sent to deliberately encourage a **flame**.

lurking Being a member of a **newsgroup** or **mailing list** and not taking an active part. Once you have made your first contribution you are no longer a lurker, even if you never **post** to the group again – there should be another word for this, but there is not one that I know of.

netiquette The generally accepted rules to follow when using the Internet, more specifically on **newsgroups**. Reading the **FAQs** on a newsgroup, if published, is good netiquette.

newbie A person new to the Internet. The term is derogatory and often aimed at users who do not follow **netiquette**.

off-list **E-mail** sent privately to a **mailing list** member is known as off-list mail.

on-list **E-mail** that is sent to be read by all **mailing list** members is known as on-list mail.

post A message mailed to a **newsgroup**.

shouting Any part of a message in CAPITALS is known as shouting. It is considered bad **netiquette** to shout a lot. Long posts that consist entirely of capitals will be ignored or will attract **flames**.

signature Lines put at the end of a **post** containing sender's name, **e-mail** address, funny quote, and other bits and pieces. It is considered bad **netiquette** to have a signature more than four or five lines long.

smiley A combination of punctuation marks that create a face when viewed sideways: :-) smile :-(sad ;-) wink {:-) smile with toupee – and many more. When making a comment that is meant to be funny, wry or ironic it is a good idea to follow it with a smiley, otherwise some readers may misconstrue your intended meaning.

spam Unwanted **e-mail** or **posts** to a **newsgroup**. Usually advertising of some kind. Hated by most Internet users – see your Internet program Help files for ways of dealing with it.

troll Someone who posts a message with deliberately incorrect information to start a flurry of messages of correction.

Some common abbreviations in newsgroups

AFAICS	As far as I can see
AFAIK	As far as I know
AFAIR	As far as I recall
AIUI	As I understand it
BTW	By the way
FWIW	For what it is worth
FYI	For your information
HAND	Have a nice day
HTH	Hope that helps
IANAL	I am not a lawyer
IIRC	If I remember correctly
IMHO	In my humble opinion
IMO	In my opinion
ISTR	I seem to remember
LOL	Laughs out loud
NG	Newsgroup
OTOH	On the other hand
PITA	Pain in the ass (i.e. a nuisance)
ROFL	Rolls on floor laughing
ROFLMAO	Rolls on floor laughing my ass off
RSN	Real soon now
RTFM	Read the 'flaming' manual
SMOP	Small matter of programming (i.e. a trivial task)
TIA	Thanks in anticipation
TTFN	Ta-ta for now
UCE	Unrequested commercial e-mail
WRT	With respect to
YMMV	Your mileage may vary (i.e. your experience may differ)

Some common file formats on the Web

For a full, and I do mean *full*, list of file formats try **www.whois.com**.

.asp Active Server Page. **Web pages** with the suffix .asp use Microsoft's version of *CGI*.

.asx A video format for Windows Media Player.

.avi A video format. You may need a **plug-in** for these files.

.cgi Common Gateway Interface. **Web pages** with the suffix .cgi will have **scripts** in them that run on the **server**. They enable the server to deal with things like forms, recording any details that you fill in, and other database activities.

.gif Graphics Interchange Format. A compact format for saving images. It was developed by CompuServe to reduce the size of image files in order to speed Internet transfer times.

.jpg or **.jpeg** Joint Photographic Experts Group. A compressed file format for images, giving faster Internet transfer times. Unlike **GIF**, JPEG is a 'lossy' format. When an image is compressed into a JPEG it loses information and therefore quality. The smaller the file is made, the less good it looks when redisplayed.

.html The suffix on the majority of **Web** files. This means that the page is written in HyperText Markup Language, a language that enables your **browser** to display the page properly on your computer screen.

.mov The format for QuickTime movie and sound files. Requires the Apple QuickTime player to be installed in your computer.

.mpg or **.mpeg** Moving Picture Experts Group. A format for video and audio files. Although much more compressed than some older formats, MPEG files are still very large and take a long time to download. MP3 is a format you will see for highly compressed, high-quality music files.

.pdf Portable Document Format. Created by Adobe, this format allows a document to be displayed exactly as the author intended, in layout, pagination and graphics, on any computer as long as Adobe Acrobat Reader is used to display it. The reader is available for different machines, PC and Mac for instance.

.ra and **.rm** Real Audio and Video. A format for files that needs the RealPlayer software to be installed in your computer.

appendices

A.1 Newsletters, communities and mailing lists

Finding lists and newsletters

E-mail lists can be good places to ask questions specific to your topic and newsletters often bring you information you would otherwise have missed. To narrow down the places specific to your subject try these two sites for a starting point:

ForumOne   http://www.forumone.com
Liszt   http://www.liszt.com

You may also carry out a search by name or category on the following sites, which carry many Web communities.

Topica   http://www.topica.com
Yahoo!   http://groups.yahoo.com

There are even mailing lists that keep you up to date with new mailing lists! Here is just one.

List-A-Day
The E-mail List Review of The Day Mailing List. To subscribe send an e-mail to **join-listaday@listaday.com** or go to the site.

http://List-A-Day.com/

What follows is an eclectic selection that should give you some idea of what flavours are available. There are thousands more lists out there. The breakdown into chapters is somewhat artificial and could be disputed, as many of the lists are not at all narrow in their aims. It was not practicable to subscribe to all of these in order to distil these aims, so I have mostly let the list moderators speak for themselves in the descriptions. You may therefore find some descriptions a little enthusiastic.

A larger selection may be found on the Website accompanying this book at **www.valley.demon.co.uk/**. The site contains over 1000 links and is regularly updated.

When you see anything in quotation marks, such as 'your-name', remember that you should insert your own details and/ or remove the quotes before using it in any message. Remember too that carets (< and >) should not be entered. Where there are no subscription instructions you can subscribe on the Website given.

General interest

IRC Undernet Writers' Page
Lots of useful resources here. Chats, critique groups, articles, links. For a free subscription send e-mail to **WritersPage-request@niestu.com** with 'subscribe' in the subject header.

http://www.getset.com/writers/

The Poetry Café
Share your poetry with friends.

http://groups.yahoo.com/group/ThePoetryCafe

SCRNWRIT
A discussion by screenwriters including script outlines, information on negotiations with agents, freelance fees and movie critiques. To subscribe send e-mail to **listserv@postal.tamu.edu** and in the body of the message put just the line 'subscribe SCRNWRIT your-name'.

Songnet
A place where songwriters and musicians can share information and specifics about songwriting.

http://groups.yahoo.com/group/Songnet

Writing techniques

Am I A Writer Yet?
The ezine for writers-to-be of all stages and ages.

http://groups.yahoo.com/group/writeryet

Article Ideas for Writers
Each week you'll receive a bounty of writing ideas targeted for your local newspapers and magazines.

http://groups.yahoo.com/community/articleideas

AuthorsDigest.com
Offers support, information and interviews of interest to working and aspiring book authors.

http://groups.yahoo.com/group/authorsdigestcom

Blackwriters-L
A discussion list for anyone interested in writing.

http://groups.yahoo.com/community/Blackwriters-L

Bye-Bye Block
A mailing list to help writers increase their skills and smash writer's block.

http://groups.yahoo.com/community/Bye-Bye_Block

The Coffeehouse Writing Perc
For a creativity jolt, caffeine-free. Receive a weekly motivational writing exercise.

http://www.coffeehouse4writers.com/perc.html

Critics
Many members of writer's lists critique each other's work. We discuss the most effective way to do that.

http://groups.yahoo.com/community/critics

Crit Pal
A free service for novelists wanting to establish critique partnerships with other novelists.

http://groups.yahoo.com/community/CritPal

Curious Quotes
A daily newsletter of entertaining and interesting quotes.

http://groups.yahoo.com/community/CuriousQuotes

Disabled Writers
A mailing list for writers of all levels who have disabilities. We discuss the unique challenges that disabled writers face.

http://groups.yahoo.com/community/DisabledWriters

E-Writers.net
A monthly newsletter for writers. Also a great resource site.

http://www.e-Writers.net

Espresso-Fiction
Welcomes all genres, but focuses on avant-garde fiction. To subscribe send e-mail to **listserv@home.ease.lsoft.com** and in the body of the message put just the line 'subscribe Espresso-Fiction your-name'.

Flash Fiction Writing Workshop
Fully worked out and polished pieces of no more than 1000 words are submitted for critique. Participation is mandatory; all members must be 18 or over and use their real names. To subscribe send e-mail to **listserv@listserv.uta** with 'subscribe Flashfiction-W' in the body of the text.

Freelance-Journalists
A list for the exchange of ideas and information about freelance journalism. To subscribe send e-mail to **majordomo@mlists.net** and in the body of the message put just the line 'subscribe free-lance-journalists'.

Humorist
A discussion list for humour writers. To subscribe send e-mail to **majordomo@nix.kconline.com** and in the body of the message put just the line 'subscribe humorist'.

IRE-L
A discussion of investigative reporting and editing techniques and training. To subscribe send e-mail to **listproc@lists.missouri.edu** and in the body of the message put just the line 'subscribe IRE-L your-name'.

Journal-writing
Discuss your journaling ideas, questions or roadblocks. This is NOT an area for online journal posting.

http://groups.yahoo.com/group/journal-writing

Magwrite
Helps published and unpublished freelance magazine writers find markets, brainstorm on articles and share their thoughts on all aspects of magazine writing. To subscribe, e-mail **listserv@maelstrom.stjohns.edu** and in the body of the message put just the line 'subscribe magwrite your-name'.

Mothers Who Write (AKA Momwrite)
An unmoderated list for stay-at-home-mothers who are also writers or who are striving to become writers. To subscribe send a blank e-mail to **momwrite-subscribe@topica.com**.

http://www.topica.com/lists/Momwrite

New Life Story Seeds
Offers inspiration and motivation for writers and journal keepers.

http://newlifestories.com

Newsmait-L
A list where journalists can discuss writing, reporting and editing. To subscribe send e-mail to **majordomo@newsmait.com** and in the body of the message put just the line 'subscribe Newsmait-L'.

Quips, Quotes and One-Liners
Great quips, quotes and one-liners sent free every weekday. To subscribe send a blank e-mail to **quips-subscribe@topica.com**.

http://www.topica.com/lists/quips

SciFi_Discussion
A mailing list for the discussion of science fiction.

http://www.topica.com/lists/SciFi_Discussion

The Sci-Fi and Fantasy Authors List
Dedicated to self-help and guidance for aspiring and successful writers in the genres of science fiction and fantasy.

http://groups.yahoo.com/group/Sci-FiAndFantasyAuth

Screen-L
Targets those who teach, research or study film and television. Discussion includes film practice, theory, history and production. To subscribe send e-mail to **listserv@ua1vm.ua.edu** and in the body of the message put just the line 'subscribe Screen-L your-name'.

Screenplay

A mailing list to discuss plays, screenplays and treatments. Discussions of current cinematic events are also welcome. For more information e-mail **sstone@primenet.com.**

http://groups.yahoo.com/group/screenplay

Sitcom

A forum for aspiring and working sitcom writers to discuss the business and writing of sitcoms. To subscribe send e-mail to **listserv@maelstrom.stjohns.edu** and in the body of the message put just the line 'subscribe Sitcom your-name'.

A Songwriter's World

A support group for songwriters worldwide to provide help in developing style and songcraft. All forms of music are welcomed. To subscribe, send a blank e-mail to **songworld-subscribe@topica.com**

http://www.topica.com/lists/songworld

TravelWritingJobs.com

A tip-filled site for those wanting to travel and get paid for it. A weekly ezine of travel writing markets and advice from Flo Conner, a full-time freelance travel writer.

http://www.travelwritingjobs.com

Two Scoops

Past columns have included how to interview your hero whether living or dead and writing your eulogy as well as suggested topics for writing.

http://www.twoscoops.com

UK-Writers

A mailing list for writers based in or writing for the UK.

http://members.tripod.com/ukwriters

Women's Words

Offers inspirational and thought-provoking quotations for women, and by women. To subscribe, e-mail **subscribe-women@send.memail.com.**

Write Advice

For writers who want to sharpen their skills or find new ways to distribute their works. To subscribe send a blank e-mail to **marie@writeadvice.abelgratis.com** with 'Yes' in the subject line.

Write Directionals

A weekly e-mail broadcast to get your writing onto paper and out the door. To subscribe send an e-mail to **majordomo @writedirectionals.com** and type 'subscribe directionals-list' in the body of the message.

http://www.WriteDirections.com

Write Lab

Bi-weekly fiction-writing exercises. After four weeks in WriteLab, you may also apply to one or more of the topics designed to assist the aspiring novelist: PlotLab, SceneLab, DraftLab, NovelsLab and MarketLab. To subscribe send e-mail to **listserv@lists.psu.edu** and in the body of the message put just the line 'subscribe WRITELAB your-name'.

Write Likely

This newsletter offers inspiration, encouragement, how-to articles and stories of failure as well as success. Also hot links, writing opportunities, subscribers' tips.

http://groups.yahoo.com/group/writelikely

The Write Thing

Offers weekly exercises, market and contest guidelines, article links on writing, author and/or editor interviews and grammar articles.

http:/groups.yahoo.com/group/writething

Writer Haven

A community for writers.

http://www.groups.yahoo.com/community/writerhaven

Writerlist

A discussion and participation list for all writers, new and established. Started by Allen Rolf and continuing after his sad death, it is both active and interesting. A nice list to start with.

http://groups.yahoo.com/group/writerlist

Writers Ink

For critiquing and commenting on works in progress, sharing support and motivation, sharing markets, contests, resources and research and participating in writing exercises and challenges.

http://writersmoon.virtualave.net/aboutwi.html

Writersclinic
A weekly mailing list for writers sharing experiences, ideas and knowledge about a new posted topic.

http://www.groups.yahoo.com/group/writersclinic

The Writing Child
For children, both writers and readers. Each bi-weekly issue features creative stories, poetry and advice from other children, as well as stories for children by adults. Work may also appear at: **http://www.geocities.com/soho/study/6219/TWChild.html**.

http://groups.yahoo.com/community/TWChild

Writing Nuggets
Short nuggets weekly; intended to inspire and instruct aspiring and professional writers.

http://groups.yahoo.com/group/writingnuggets

WSF (Women's Short Fiction)
A list for writers of fiction stories that are of interest mainly to women. To subscribe send e-mail to **majordomo@majordomo.net** and in the body of the message put just the line 'subscribe WSF'.

Research

Find Law
Now offering daily e-mail delivery of Federal Regulations and Public Laws News updates.

http://www.findlaw.com

Fireseek Literary Arts Site Update
Editors, moderators and visitors find the hottest literary sites on the Net. To subscribe, pick your category at the site, enter your e-mail address and press join.

http://www.fireseek.com

Freebies for Writers
Each issue includes an in-depth collection of sources for research materials.

http://groups.yahoo.com/community/freebiesforwriters

Historical Research
A list for people who research historical novels in all genres.

http://groups.yahoo.com/community/historicalresearch

Library Spot Newsletter
Points out the latest and greatest reference tools, online libraries, periodicals and online texts. Monthly.
http://www.libraryspot.com/newsletter.htm

The Muse's Muse Songwriting Resource
An excellent resource for songwriters. To subscribe to its free monthly newsletter, send e-mail to **majordomo@samurai.com** with 'subscribe musesnews' in the message body.

Rob's wURLd 'Best of the Web'
This is one of the best reports for most information sources. Whole groups of sites are themed by subject. Past issues are archived.
http://RobswURLd.listbot.com/

URMA-L
The university research magazines list. To subscribe send e-mail to **listserv@lists.psu.edu** and in the body of the message put just the line 'subscribe URMA-L your-name'.

Publishing and books

Publisher related

AAP
The Association of Authors and Publishers focuses on producing, developing, marketing and distributing books. To subscribe, send e-mail to **majordomo@authorsandpublishers.org** and in the body of the message put just the line 'subscribe AAP'.

PUB-Forum
The Publishers Forum is a list for small and independent publishers.
http://groups.yahoo.com/group/pub-forum

Publish
A discussion list for struggling, self-publishing writers.
http://groups.yahoo.com/community/publish

Scribe-LIST
A resource for writers' issues, including self-publishing and ghostwriting. To subscribe send e-mail to **scribe-list-request @bellicose.com** and in the subject line put 'subscribe'.

Secrets of Self-Publishing Success

For people who want to write a book and publish it themselves. To subscribe send an e-mail to **Subscribe@zinfo.net** and include your name in the body of the message.

Web Builder Newsletter

Website design and development.

http://www.Website-designs.com/out.html

Ezines

EzineLinks

A discussion list where ezine and newsletter promotion tips, links, exchanges and ideas are discussed and promoted. To subscribe send an e-mail to **join_ezinelinks@sendfree.com** and include the subject heading 'NewList'.

http://www.andersoncreations.com/subscribe.shtml

EZU Journal

Aims to keep you up to date on the latest happenings in ezine publishing.

http://www.ezineuniversity.com

Zine Directory

A mailing list to discuss, review, announce and join ezines.

http://groups.yahoo.com/group/ZineDirectory

E-book related

An E-book Chat

A mailing list for writers wanting to publish an e-book.

http://groups.yahoo.com/community/AnEBookChat

E-book Junction

EJ reviews e-books (free or for sale) and offers interviews with authors. Writing and e-publishing resources, news and links to sites for research and advice are also provided.

http://www.atlanticbridge.net/pubs/ebookjunction.htm

ebook-List

A forum devoted to the discussion of all topics related to e-book authoring, publishing, marketing and reading. To subscribe send an e-mail to **majordomo@exemplary.net** with 'subscribe ebook-list' in the body of the message.

Ebook net
Newsletter for e-books and e-publishing. Also a great site to visit for information.

http://www.ebooknet.com

The e-books Listserv
Set up to discuss the design, sales and marketing of e-books, e-publishing and the like, this is also the area to discuss topics from the Website **http://www.booklocker.com**.

http://groups.yahoo.com/community/eBooks

Book related

Art and lies
A mailing list for those who love real literature.

http://groups.yahoo.com/group/artandlies

Book Spot Newsletter
This newsletter points out the latest and greatest sites for book reviews, stores, news, events, reading lists, author and publisher information, and more.

http://www.bookspot.com/newsletter.htm

Christian-bookreview
Read any good books lately? If you hated it, tell us why. If you loved it, then recommend it to someone else. All books must be representative of Jesus Christ whether fiction or not.

http://groups.yahoo.com/group/christian-bookreview

Cookbook Reviews
Looking for the best cookbook for a particular cuisine? Just ask.

http://groups.yahoo.com/group/cookbook-reviews

Destellae Sci-Fi/Fantasy
A mailing list for the discussion of science fiction and fantasy. For more information, contact Brett Chapman at **brettc@ihug.co.nz**.

http://www.destellae.somewhere.net

Eclectics
A quarterly newsletter to promote authors and their latest releases. To subscribe send an e-mail to **e-newsletter@eclectics.com** and put 'subscribe' in the subject line.

http://www.eclectics.com

In the First
A modern crime fiction discussion group mainly concerned with hard-boiled fiction.

http://groups.yahoo.com/community/inthefirst

Literary News & Notes Tip of the Day
Features interesting news items, tips and observations about the world of letters.

http://www.tipworld.com

Media
Focuses on journalism in Europe. To subscribe send e-mail to **listserv@psychology.su.se** and in the body of the message put just the line 'subscribe media your-name'.

Mystery
A mailing list for the discussion of spy/mystery/private detective/police books – fiction and non-fiction.

http://groups.yahoo.com/community/mystery

Quaker Books for Friends
Monthly eclectic reviews of books of interest to Christian Friends.

http://QuakerBooks.listbot.com

Readers and writers
Discuss and recommend books. Exchange writings and, upon request, constructive criticism will be given by at least one person.

http://groups.yahoo.com/group/Readersandwriters

Romance Books Exchange
Exchange used romance books with other romance lovers.

http://www.groups.yahoo.com/group/RomanceBooksExchange

Twilight Times
Ezine of speculative fiction. Featuring well-written fiction and poetry from some of the best Net writers. Practical Tips for Online Authors monthly column.

http://www.twilighttimes.com

Victorian Fiction
A forum for people who love Victorian fiction and love to read and/or write it.

http://groups.yahoo.com/group/VictorianFiction

Word of Mouth Book Blurbs
A newsletter focusing on e-books and print-on-demand titles.

http://www.xcpublishing.com/wompage.html

Marketing related

Authors Online
Valuable information designed to help authors or publishers market their books more effectively.

http://www.seekbooks.com/opt_in_m.htm

Bookmarket
Focuses on marketing and promoting books. To subscribe send e-mail to **majordomo@bookzone.com** and in the body of the message put just the line 'subscribe bookmarket'.

Online Advertising
A discussion of strategies, results, studies and media coverage of online advertising. To subscribe send e-mail to **online-ads-request@o-a.com** and in the body of the message put just the word 'subscribe'.

Writing opportunites

The 21st Century Publishing Update
A newsletter for authors, small presses and self-publishers.

http://www.groups.yahoo.com/group/WritePublish

Article Submission E-Gazette
Bi-weekly newsletter. How to be a freelance writer and where to find paying markets.

http://mjvn.co.za/hd/article.htm

Bluedog Société
A list for authors, orators, poets and writers to submit their writing for publishing on the Internet. To subscribe send e-mail to **majordomo@armchair.mb.ca** and in the body of the message put just the line 'subscribe bluedogsociete'.

Journalism, editing and other disciplines

Copyediting-L
Focuses on matters related to editing: style issues; newspaper, technical and other specialized editing; reference books; client

relations; Internet resources; electronic editing and software; freelance issues; and so on. To subscribe send e-mail to **listserv@listserv.indiana.edu** and in the body of the message put just the line 'subscribe copyediting-L your-name'.

Euroscribes
A community for European and Europe-based journalists to debate issues and trends, help each other in their work and commiserate. To join Euroscribes send a blank e-mail to **blueear-euroscribes-subscribe @egroups.com**.

The Freelance Journalists
A mailing list for freelance journalists.

http://groups.yahoo.com/list/freelancejourn/info.html

Intcar-L
Covers computer-assisted reporting from an international perspective. To subscribe send e-mail to **listserv@american.edu** and in the body of the message put just the line 'subscribe Intcar-L your-name'.

Online-News
Covers online newspapers and magazines and general journalism. To subscribe send e-mail to **lyris@planetarynews.com** and in the body of the message put just the line 'subscribe Online-News'.

TECHWR-L
The Technical Writers List is a forum for all technical communication issues. To subscribe send e-mail to **listserv@listserv.okstate.edu** and in the body of the message put just the line 'subscribe TECHWR-L your-name'.

TVIDEA
A forum for television writers, producers, reporters and editors to exchange story ideas. To subscribe send e-mail to **majordomo@indra.com** and in the body of the message put just the line 'subscribe TVIDEA'.

General industry

Byte Out of Crime
A bi-monthly resource for content Web writers. Postings of positive and negative dealings with Websites, by other writers, provide information regarding the payment history of Web owners.

http://www.groups.yahoo.com/community/byteoutofcrime

NASW-Freelance

A list for freelance science writers run by the National Association of Science Writers. To subscribe send e-mail to **majordomo@nasw.org** and in the body of the message put just the line 'subscribe NASW-Freelance'.

NWU-CHAT

The National Writers Union's discussion list. To subscribe send e-mail to **majordomo@igc.org** and in the body of the message put just the line 'subscribe NWU-CHAT'.

SPJ-L

The Society of Professional Journalists' list. To subscribe send e-mail to **listserv@psuvm.psu.edu** and in the body of the message put just the line 'subscribe SPJ-L your-name'.

Jobs

Freelancehelp.com

A site where freelancers can find work.

http://www.freelancehelp.com

Freelance Success

Detailed market information and online writing classes for non-fiction writers. E-mail **freelance-success@usa.net** for more details.

http://www.freelancesuccess.com

Oasis-l

A mailing list for Cyber Oasis, a monthly newsletter that connects subscribers to the best resources on the Net for writers and readers. It offers links to many articles, original material and a jobs board.

http://www.sunoasis.com/oasis.html

Work for writers

Writing job mailing list.

http://groups.yahoo.com/community/workforwriters

Writers Unite

Promoting networking and paying markets for writers.

http://www.geocities.com/lisa_mason2001/Writeforthewebhome.html

A.2 Site lists

For many more sites (over 1000) visit the Website that accompanies this book at **www.valley.demon.co.uk/**

01 Overview of the Internet

General

Access Internet Magazine
Website with a database of more than 3000 reviewed sites.
http://www.accessmagazine.com

Inscriptions
Excellent weekly ezine for professional writers.
http://www.inscriptionsmagazine.com/

The Victory Page For Fiction Writers
Guides on critiquing, advice for joining online writing groups and how to overcome writer's block. Links. Some good advice for the beginner.
http://www.crayne.com/

Chat

IRC Undernet Writers' Page
Lots of useful resources here with chats, critique groups, articles, links. For a free newsletter subscription, send an e-mail to **WritersPage-request@niestu.com** with 'subscribe' in the subject header or visit the site.
http://www.getset.com/writers/

Communities
Geocities Communities
Many communities and links.
http://www.geocities.com/

iAgora
A virtual community. Links to many iAgora sites worldwide with forums.
http://www.iagora.com

02   Writing techniques

Children's writing

Children's Book Council
A resource for writers and illustrators of children's literature.
http://www.cbcbooks.org/

Children's Publisher Guidelines
Resource site for children's writers and illustrators. Publisher submission guidelines links.
http://www.signaleader.com/chldwrit.html

Children's Writing Resource Center
A Website for children's writers with many links, articles and FAQs.
http://www.write4kids.com/index.html

Editing

Editors' and Writers' Toolkit
This is a good reference site with links and tookits for the business of writing – a journalist's, a book-lover's and a women's history toolkit. Among others!
http://writetools.com/

Elements of Style
William Strunk Jr's classic grammar guide is available online, along with many other reference books.
http://www.bartleby.com/141/index.html

The Slot: A Spot for Copy Editors
This site will answer most of your copyediting questions.
http://www.theslot.com

Fiction

Book Marc
Adventures in fiction writing techniques from Peter E. Abresch. Excellent articles.
http://www.olg.com/pfwriter/

Eclectics.com
Articles on settings, synopses, creating characters, romance.
http://www.eclectics.com/articles.html

Fiction Factor

Articles on the craft of fiction writing and tips for getting your work published. Alerts and warnings about publishers who take advantage of writers' articles. Some magazine guidelines.

http://www.fictionfactor.com

Fiction Fix

Articles, essays and features on writing.

http://fictionfix.tripod.com

The Fiction Writer's Page

Articles on: story elements, style, plot, synopsis, genre, voice, dialogue, character, publishers, contracts and agents.

http://www.capcollege.bc.ca/magic/cmns/fwp.html

Painted Rock

Reputable classes for fiction writing. Back issues with helpful articles on writing techniques.

http://www.paintedrock.com

Pure Fiction

A site for both writers and readers. Articles and a good list of UK publishers.

http://www.purefiction.co.uk/

Fiction Writer's Resource

Agents, ideas, tips, and more.

http://www.geocities.com/SoHo/Nook/9082/writersresources.html

General

1001 links

Boasting 1001 links to articles about fiction writing, a huge amount of information is accessible.

http://www.angelfire.com/va/storyguide/

The Editor's Pen

Another excellent site for advice and further links.

http://www.pathway.net/dwlacey

e-Writers.Net

Over a hundred pages of writing information. Start at this page.

http://e-writers.net/outline.html

Goin SOHO
Links to work-at-home resources plus tips on surviving the Small HOme Office.

http://goinsoho.com

John Hewitt's Writer's Resource Center
A resource-rich site for writers, editors and journalists. The FAQ Center is good.

http://www.poewar.com

Mike Barker's Writers' Exercises
Hundreds of exercises for you. Also writing links.

http://Web.mit.edu/mbarker/www/exercises/exercises.html

Published!
How To Reach Writing Success: useful articles and resources from *Inklings* columnist Marcia Yudkin. Visit this and bookmark it.

http://www.yudkin.com/publish.htm

Query Letter Information
Links to a number of splendid articles on query letter writing.

http://www.accelnet.com/victoria/queries2.html

SharpWriter.Com
Writers' resources. Articles and links. I loved 'Copyright Piracy: It Happened to Me!'

http://www.sharpwriter.com

Suite 101
Good writers' site.

http://www.suite101.com

Tips For Writers
Moira Allen's Web resource for writers. Lots of useful articles, from basic writing to selling and publishing. Some good links.

http://www.tipsforwriters.com

UCLA
Online writing classes.

http://www.onlinelearning.net/

University of Illinois Writer's Workshop
Excellent resource. Links to a grammar handbook, writing tips, advice on getting your critiques, resources for writing teachers, writing resources, and much more.
http://www.english.uiuc.edu/cws/wworkshop/index.htm

WGA Writers' Index
Many good links for writers.
http://www.wga.org/forwriters_index.html

Word Museum
Online writing classes and much more.
http://www.wordmuseum.com

Writers Club University
Online writing classes and more.
http://www.writersclub.com/wcu/catalog.cfm

Writer's Digest
A wealth of information, articles and links.
http://www.writersdigest.com

Writer Exchange
Writing-related articles, creativity-boosting tips, publishing links plus a literary agent directory covering fiction, non-fiction and screenplays.
http://writerexchange.about.com/arts/writerexchange/

Writing Help for Parents
Articles, links and contest information.
http://www.suite101.com/welcome.cfm/writing_help_for_parents

Writers Review
Author interviews, fiction help and article advice. Plus 'rooms' for various writing genres in which you can find some really cool things.
http://www.writersreview.com

Writers Write
Good writers' resource.
http://www.writerswrite.com

Screenwriting

Drew's Script-O-Rama
Hundreds of links to scripts: shooting scripts, drafts, unused scripts and transcripts for major movies and TV shows. See how the pros do it and learn.

http://www.script-o-rama.com

The Screenwriter In Cyberspace
A regular column by Charles Deemer and an archive of past columns.

http://Screenwriters.com/Deemer/

Screenwriting
Articles, links, a review of Movie Magic Screenwriter software and more.

http://screenwriting.about.com/arts/screenwriting/

03   Web search engines

Here are a few specialist sites. For the major ones see Chapter 3.

AV Photo Finder
Enter your keywords and find a picture. A good resource. This site is also reachable from the main Alta Vista page.

http://www.altavista.com/cgi-bin/query?mmdo=1&stype=simage

Beaucoup!
Research a wide range of subjects.

http://www.beaucoup.com

Dogpile
Yes, I know! But it's a good search engine.

http://dogpile.com

Google
This page searches on government Web pages.

http://www.google.com/unclesam

MagOmania.com
A Canadian-based magazine search engine.

http://www.magomania.com

Molesearch
An engine dedicated to the many aspects of publishing.
http://www.molesearch.com

The US Copyright Office
A Web-based search engine to locate the copyright status of millions of books, music recordings, movies and software items. Copyright records held date back to 1978.
http://www.loc.gov/copyright/search

Meta-search engines

Meta-search engine sites or sites for downloading meta-search programs.

All-One-Search
This is the big hit using over 500 engines. Here you will find the engine for your specialized search.
http://www.allonesearch.com

Copernic
Site for downloading a meta-search program that runs on your computer.
http://www.copernic.com

Ixquick
An excellent, fast meta-search engine that searches 14 engines at once. Can use advanced Boolean searches, working out which of the engines it is using can handle them.
http://www.ixquick.com

SearchIQ
Links to many engines. It suggests which might be best for your type of search.
http://www.zdnet.com/searchiq/

Web Ferret
Home of a suite of programs that help in Web searches.
http://www.zdnet.com/ferret/index.html

Search engine news
Sites that help you keep up with changes to search engines.

Notess
A good site for search engine information and news.
http://www.notess.com

The Search Engine Watch
Keep up to date with news of search engine changes. Also holds good information on engines.
http://www.searchenginewatch.com

04   Internet Research

Library and university sites

CNNfyi
From CNN, a news and educational site for students and teachers. News researched and reported by students.
http://fyi.cnn.com/fyi/

The Comprehensive Digital Reference Service
A consortium of the world's top libraries, including Yale, Harvard, Cornell, the US National Gallery and the national libraries of Canada and Australia.
http://www.loc.gov/rr/digiref/

LibWeb
Links to worldwide libraries. This is another one to bookmark.
http://sunsite.Berkeley.edu/LibWeb/

University Libraries
Online catalogues of available research material. Links to contributing libraries.
http://copac.ac.uk/copac

Dictionaries and encyclopaedias

1 Look Dictionaries
More than 200 online dictionaries and glossaries. If you can't find it here, you probably never will.
http://www.onelook.com/browse.shtml

Bartleby.com
Dictionaries, the complete unabridged *Cambridge History of*

English and American Literature, the *Columbia Encyclopaedia*, a thesaurus and a selection of classic books.
http://www.bartleby.com

British–American–British Dictionary
Two nations divided by a single language.
http://www.peak.org/~jeremy/dictionary/dict.html

Columbia
The concise *Columbia Encyclopaedia*.
http://www.encyclopedia.com

The Internet Public Library
A reference section, e-texts and good links.
http://ipl.sils.umich.edu or http://www.ipl.org

Law.com
A legal dictionary search engine.
http://www.law.com

Oxford English Dictionary
Access to the home of the English language is expensive at the moment. Expect the price to be reduced at some point. Live in hope that one day it might even be free.
http://www.oed.com

Plumb Design Visual Thesaurus
Interactive thesaurus, by clicking on words you can follow a thread of meaning. Intriguing.
http://www.plumbdesign.com/thesaurus/

The Semantic Rhyming Dictionary
An online program that finds a rhyme to most words.
http://www.link.cs.cmu.edu/cgi-bin/dougb/rhyme.cgi

Research starting points

Awesome Library
'14,000 carefully reviewed resources' is the claim. A good starting point for any research, with 24 basic categories that further sub-divide. This is in my bookmarks and will stay there.
http://www.awesomelibrary.org

Finding Data On The Internet
A journalist's guide. Some good sites linked.
http://www.robertniles.com/data/

History Research Online
Terrific research site with many links.
http://members.aol.com/historyresearch

A Journalist's Guide To The Internet
Maintained by the University of Maryland.
http://reporter.umd.edu/

The Journalist's Toolbox
3500 Website links helpful to anyone working in the media.
http://www.journaliststoolbox.com

Mystery Writers' Resources
A huge list of links, many of them to stuff you'll need to know
if you plan to kill someone (in a book!).
http://www.zott.com/mysforum/links.htm

Needle in a CyberStack InfoFinder
The 'needle navigator' takes you to a good selection of resources.
http://members.home.net/albeej/

Noah Says
'That this is a place to turn to for all of our How to and What
is questions.'
http://www.noahsays.com

Ref Desk
Where does one begin with a site like this? Search the site, the
Web, the dictionary or newsgroups. It has links to so many
good resources that all I can say is bookmark it. I have.
http://www.refdesk.com/

Reporter's Internet Guide
Hundreds of links for working journalists.
http://www.crl.com:80/~jshenry/rig.html

Resource page of the Library of Congress
Has many links to research tools that you will find useful.
http://lcWeb.loc.gov/rr/news/othint.html

SciCentral.com
Online science resources plus an e-mail news alert.
http://www.scicentral.com

Sources
One of the best source-finders on the Internet with over 5000 experts and media contacts. Although mostly Canadian in content it is still well worth a visit wherever you live.
http://www.sources.com

Travel Writing
Lots of resources at this travel writing site.
http://www.suite101.com/welcome.cfm/travel_writing

WISDOM: Knowledge and Literature Search
Links to valuable writing sites and literature sites.
http://thinkers.net/

WWWScribe
Writers resources with emphasis on Web searching, authoring and e-mail.
http://www.wwwscribe.com/

05 Electronic publishing

Book Zone Pro
A terrific Website of publishing resources. Lists of specialized industry resources, recent publishing news and polls, experts to answer questions, useful articles, recent job listings and a reviewer database to help promote your latest book.
http://bookzonepro.com

Literary agents

AAR
Association of Authors Representatives FAQ for tips on how to query an agent.
http://www.publishersweekly.com/aar/FAQs.html

Agent Research and Evaluation
Submit an agent's name for a reputation sketch. Complete reports on agents and scams are available for a fee. This URL

leads to the verification page of the site.

http://www.agentresearch.com/agent_ver.html

Literary Agent.Com
Search engine for finding agents.

http://nt9.nyic.com/literaryagent/sch-page.html

UK Literary Agents
A list of UK agents with addresses and a brief description of their specialities.

http://www.ibmpcug.co.uk/~fiction/pages/agents.htm

The Writers' Exchange Literary Agent Directory
A listing of literary agents with contact information, e-mail addresses and URLs.

http://writerexchange.about.com/library/agents/blagentdir.htm

E-publishers

General

The Directory of eBook Publishers
Search and locate royalty-paying companies affiliated with the Electronically Published Professionals Organization. Each listing presents a link to the e-publishers site, an example of a current book or imprint and a description of the publisher's wants and needs.

http://www.thewisdomkeeper.com/director.htm

Ebook Connections
A good site with lots of articles and links to many e-book publishers.

http://www.ebookconnections.com

Ebook Net
A good site for general industry information. Many links and good articles.

http://www.ebooknet.com

Children's

Klocke Publishing
Parent and child-oriented e-publisher. Free books and resource links onsite.

http://www.klockepresents.com

Word Wrangler Publishing
eKIDnas are electronic books for children published in the TK3 reader format. Reader download is free.
http://www.wordwrangler.com

Dark fiction

MOT Press
Masters of Terror print publishers Read the opening of a print book before purchase.
http://members.aol.com/andyfair/motpress.html

Educational

Questia
For the cost of one printed text book, students can access an unlimited amount of Questia's 50,000 titles from 135 publishers.
http://www.Questia.com

Gay

GLB Publishers
E-publishers for gays, lesbians and bisexuals.
http://www.glbpubs.com/

Multi-genre

Cayuse Press
Publishers' Website with many links.
http://www.cayuse-press.com/index.html

DiskUs Publishing
E-publisher.
http://www.diskuspublishing.com

Eastgate Systems
Hypertext literature.
http://www.eastgate.com

eBook Heaven
A bookstore for electronic books.
http://www.stormpages.com/ebookheaven

ebooksonthe.net
E-book club.

http://www.ebooksonthe.net

Fiction Works
E-book publisher.

http://www.fictionworks.com/

Hard Shell Word Factory
A very busy multi-genre e-publisher. Has an e-book bestseller list with links to download sites.

http://www.hardshell.com

Mind's Eye Fiction
A new publishing idea: read the start of a story and if you want to finish it pay a small fee or opt for a free version containing ads.

http://tale.com/

NexusTeq Publications
Royalty paying e-publisher of fiction and non-fiction.

http://ebooks.nexusteq.com

Renaissance E Books
E-publisher specializing in multi-genre novels and erotica.

http://renebooks.com

Speculation Press
Print publisher offering the first 25 pages of books of 'speculative fiction' to read before purchase.

http://www.speculationpress.com

Twilight Times Books
E-publisher. Recently offered its first shareware e-book.

http://www.twilighttimes.com

Word Wrangler
Multi-genre e-book publisher.

http://www.wordwrangler.com

Wordbeams
Multi-genre e-publisher. Guidelines supplied.

http://www.wordbeams.com

Poetry

Wordcircuits
A showcase for hypertext poetry and fiction.
http://www.wordcircuits.com/gallery

Romance

Heart Realm
Romance books.
http://www.heartrealm.com

iReadRomance.com
An e-publisher. Join the iRR club and get sent a monthly newsletter and free stories. Quite a lot more onsite.
http://www.iReadRomance.com

Fantasy/Science fiction

Baen Books
Publisher offers science fiction e-books in electronic format. For $10 per month, readers will get four books before they are available in print.
http://www.baen.com

Del Rey Books
Fantasy and science fiction.
http://www.randomhouse.com/delrey

Women

DLSIJ Press
E-publisher of women authors.
http://www.dlsijpress.com

E-publishing resources

e-books Plus Web Ring
Resource for authors and publishers of electronic books.
http://www.angelfire.com/in2/ebooksPlusWebRing/index.html

Publicity Depot
A publicity resource for authors.
http://www.PublicityDepot.com

Publisher List Site
Brief description of publishers worldwide and links to their Websites.
http://www.lights.com/publisher/

Ezines

For further ezines look at *Ezine Search* and *Ezines Database*.
http://ezinesearch.com and http://www.infojump.com

Children

The Writing Parent
Ezine for writing parents and carers.
http://www.klockepresents.com/

Educational

Family Tree Magazine
Aims to help beginner/intermediate genealogists with their family history.
http://www.familytreemagazine.com

Gay

QT Magazine.com
An online gay and lesbian travel magazine.
http://www.qtmagazine.com

Health

Men's Health Magazine
Exactly what it says.
http://www.Menshealth.com

PrimeSeason.com
Health ezine for the over 40s with a genealogy section.
http://www.primeseason.com

History

Of Ages Past Magazine
Ezine geared to historical fiction.
http://www.angelfire.com/il/ofagespast

Pivotal Glyph
'A time capsule of American contemporary history and culture.'

http://www.pivotalglyph.com

Dark fiction

Alsirat
Horror anthology.

http://www.alsirat.com/alsirat.html

Dark Echo
This ezine was awarded a Bram Stoker Award for Superior Achievement in Horror. Stories, articles and links.

http://www.darkecho.com

Humour

Private Eye
British satirical magazine. Around so long it has become almost part of the establishment. Wickedly funny.

http://www.private-eye.co.uk

The Wacky Times
Online humour newspaper 'Following in the grand tradition of journalism by not letting the truth get in the way of news.' For when you deserve a break.

http://www.wackytimes.com

Journals

Meta Journals
Ezine about the online journals.

http://www.metajournals.com/main.html

Personal Journaling
An ezine for journal writers.

http://www.writersdigest.com/journaling/

Lifestyle

Hope
An ezine providing 'good news' and inspirational stories.

http://mountainmist.designspot.com/Hope.html

Men

Maxim Magazine
An ezine for men.
http://www.maxim-magazine.co.uk

Men's Journal
Adventure, travel, sports, fitness, ideas.
http://www.mensjournal.com

Multi-genre

Dreamwords
A literary ezine. Poetry, quotes, anecdotes and humour.
http://www.angelfire.com/in/dreamwords

Electronic Tales
Serial stories in several genres. Instalments are e-mailed five times a week.
http://www.electronictales.com

Palimpsest
Ezine for short stories.
http://www.chuchin.com/palimpsest/

Reach Out Magazine
Ezine with stories, humour and anecdotes related to the disabled community.
http://www.reachoutmag.com

The Running River Reader
For readers of e-books. Includes profiles of e-book authors and where to find their books.
http://www.runningriver.com

Mystery

Smort
Host of the Mystery and Suspense Writer's Workshop
http://www.smort.com

The Thrilling Detective
Stories, reviews and much more.
http://www.colba.net/~kvnsmith/thrillingdetective/index.html

Poetry

Dark Angel Poetry Magazine
A British ezine.
http://www.angelfire.com/id/Darkangel2

Mind Fire
Poetry journal with poems, articles, bios and links.
http://www.kakuta.com/mindfire

Romance

Amore Magazine
Short story romance.
http://www.amoremagazine.com

The Harlequin Romance.Net
The ultimate online destination for romantic escape.
http://www.eHarlequin.com

Fantasy/Science fiction

Fantasy Folklore and Fairytales
International fantasy ezine.
http://www.Fantasytoday.com

Morbid Musings
An e-zine dedicated to horror and dark fantasy.
http://www.meghansmusings.com/morbid.html

Pulp Fantasy
SF, fantasy, horror and anime ezine.
http://www.pulpfantasy.com

Travel

Travel Writers.com
A resource for travel writers. A guide to the best resources for travel writers, up-to-date market information and tips for improving your writing when you register.
http://travelwriters.com

Women

Concerning Women
A free information resource concerning issues of today's woman.
http://www.concerningwomen.com

Dish Magazine
An ezine for 'young women of all ages'.
http://www.dishmag.com

Ezine resources

Am I A Writer Yet?
A free monthly writing ezine.
http://groups.yahoo.com/community/writeryet

Fiction Online
An index of online fiction magazines and authors.
http://www.angelfire.com/zine2/fictiononline

Writer's Exchange
Writing community and ezine with market opportunities.
http://www.ozemail.com.au/~pjcsjc/writers-exchange/exchange.htm

Writers Mirror
UK-based ezine. Reports, articles and resources.
http://www.manninWeb.co.im/writer/wmirror.html

Booksellers and book reviews

Americanabooks.com
An online discount book store also with e-books. A feature allows readers to bid on what they believe should be the price of a book.
http://www.americanabooks.com

Book Closeouts
Bargain books and remainders.
http://www.bookcloseouts.com

The Book Exchange
Trade/swap/exchange books Mostly general fiction.
http://groups.yahoo.com/subscribe.cgi/BookExchange

Book Pricer
Search engine for book buyers. Finds a book at the best price – new, used and out of print.
http://www.bookpricer.com

Book Reporter
Many-featured site. Latest novels reviewed, author interviews and 'The Week in Book History' and the 'Books Into Movies' sections.
http://www.bookreporter.com

BookBrowse
Brings you excerpts of the best current books, plus summaries, reviews and author bios.
http://www.bookbrowse.com/

BookZone
Books and links from 1200 professional publishers.
http://www.bookzone.com

EBookShoppe.com
Scribblers bookstore selling e-books.
http://www.ebookshoppe.com

Evenbetter!com
An online bookstore book price comparison search engine.
http://www.acses.com

net Library
A collection of free e-books and a selection that may be viewed online or downloaded.
http://www.netlibrary.com

Popula
A Web auction service specializing in collectible books.
http://www.popula.com

The Word Pool
UK children's books with author profiles, ideas to get kids reading and book reviews organized by topic instead of age group.
http://www.wordpool.co.uk

Write4kids

Offers a free e-book for children's writers: *Secrets of Writing Great Picture Books.*

http://www.write4kids.com/ebooks.html

Guidelines

Magazine Writers' Net
Website with advice on publishing and more.

http://magwriters.virtualave.net/

Speculative Fiction Markets

http://www.cs.cmu.edu/~mslee/mag.html

Writer's Digest
Paying markets, guidelines and publishing news. Home of Writer's Market.

http://www.writersdigest.com/guidelines/index.htm

Writer's Guidelines Database
A huge database of publications and guidelines.

http://mav.net/guidelines/

The Writer's Place
650+ market guidelines.

http://www.awoc.com

Opportunities

Correspondent.com
Website for freelance journalists. A chance to market your work globally.

http://www.correspondent.com

FreelanceWriting.com
A magazine guideline database of paying markets.

http://www.freelancewriting.com/guidelines/pages

The Write Markets Report
Free newsletter with freelance job listings and paying markets.

http://www.writersmarkets.com

General industry Websites, services and writers' organizations

The Association of Electronic Publishers

A self-policing organization assuring that 'a member of AEP is a trustworthy publisher'.

http://welcome.to/AEP

Association of Investigative Journalists

The organization aims to 'encourage greater use of, and discussion about, investigative journalism amongst journalists, producers, editors and other professionals.'

http://www.aij-uk.com

Authors Licensing and Collecting Society UK

Register online for revenue from licensed photocopying of your work.

http://www.alcs.co.uk/

The Authors Studio

Association of small press owning authors. Aids members with printing, distribution, marketing and intellectual rights.

http://www.theauthorsstudio.org/

British Guild of Travel Writers

Self-explanatory.

http://ourworld.compuserve.com/homepages/BGTW/

The Electronic Authors Guild International

Aims to help the e-book author.

http://www.eguild.org

The Guild of Food Writers

The professional association of food writers and broadcasters in the UK.

http://www.gfw.co.uk/index.html

IndyPublish

The global community of independent authors.

http://www.indypublish.com/home.htm

National Writers Union Website

The union for freelancers working in the US market.

http://www.nwu.org

NUJ
Home of the British National Union of Journalists.
http://www.gn.apc.org/media/nuj.html

Publishers Weekly
The industry bible in the USA. Take a look at this one.
http://www.publishersweekly.com/

Scholarly Electronic Publishing
Bibliography with close to 1000 articles and books on electronic publishing.
http://info.lib.uh.edu/sepb/sepb.html

SFEP (Society of Freelance Editors and Proofreaders)
Has a directory of members' services and links. Over 1400 members.
http://www.sfep.org.uk/

Society of Authors UK
Several thousand authors are represented by the Society.
http://www.writers.org.uk/society/

World Romance Writers
Non-profit organization for the promotion of romance writers around the world.
http://www.worldromancewriters.com

Writer Beware
If you can see the sea breaking on the reef, you stand a better chance of coming through unscathed. This site shows you the breakers.
http://www.sfwa.org/Beware/Warnings.html

Writers Guild of America
The WGA is the union representing writers in the motion picture, broadcast, cable and new media industries.
East: http://www.wgaeast.org/
West: http://www.wga.org/

Writers Guild of Great Britain
http://www.writers.org.uk/guild/

06   Serious matters

Jobs

AJR Newslink/Joblink
The American Journalism Review. For reporters, copy editors, freelancers and more.

http://ajr.newslink.org/x-joblink.html

Authorlink! Classifieds
This is a good source for freelance assignments. Don't be put off by a short list. It's updated twice a month and you'll need to come back.

http://www.authorlink.com/jobs.html

Avalanche of Jobs
Jobs are plucked mainly from newsgroups so there are many poor ones to sift through. Some look good though.

http://www.sunoasis.com/freelance.html

Global Telecommute
For people interested in working as telecommuters.

http://www.globaltelecommute.com

HowToWeb Jobs
A job database for Internet professionals.

http://www.howtowebjobs.com

The Monster Board
A large selection of jobs in many disciplines. Writing jobs seem to come under arts. You can set up an 'agent' for job types and get informed when new jobs come in. First site is US only.

http://jobsearch.monster.com/
http://international.monster.com/search/

Talent Cue
A directory for UK freelancers in the communications industry.

http://www.talentcue.com

Technical Writing
Jobs, discussions, links and networking.

http://www.writerswrite.com/technical

The Write Jobs
Jobs for Writers.
http://www.writerswrite.com/jobs/

Writing Employment Center
Frequently updated. Job postings, job-hunting tips, articles and many other resources. Highly recommended.
http://www.poewar.com/jobs.htm

Security

Internet Fraud
Advice on how to stay safe when on the Internet.
http://www.internet-fraud.co.uk

PGP
Interoperability information and advice.
http://www.turnpike.com/pgpadvice.html

Virus FAQ
Great virus details.
http://www.alw.nih.gov/Security/FIRST/papers/virus/faq.txt

Dr Solomon
Virus detection and repair program download site.
http://www.drsolomon.com/

McAfee
Virus detection and repair program download site.
http://www.mcafee.com/

Norton
Virus detection and repair program download site.
http://www.symantec.com/

Copyright

Take care that you know whether you are looking at British or American law. There are some differences.

A Novice Writer's Guide To Rights
Article.
http://www.writerswrite.com/journal/dec97/cew3.htm

Copyright & Fair Use
Advice from Stanford University.
http://fairuse.stanford.edu/

The Copyright Website
Articles and links.
http://www.benedict.com/

Internet copyright FAQs
http://www.faqs.org/

LexisONE
A Website combining free case law and legal forms.
http://www.lexisone.com

Templeton's 10 Big Copyright Myths
http://www.templetons.com/brad/copymyths.html

US Copyright Office on US Copyright Law
http://lcWeb.loc.gov/copyright/title17/

US Register of Copyrights
http://www.loc.gov/copyright/onlinesp

Web Law FAQ
http://www.patents.com/Weblaw.sht

Just for fun

Andy's Anagram Solver
Great for crossword enthusiasts. Now available in French too!
http://www.ssynth.co.uk/~gay/anagram.html

Brain Candy
Insults, riddles, jokes, humour, wordplay, mind games.
http://www.corsinet.com/braincandy/index.html

The Internet Conspiracy Generator
Tired of reading the same old conspiracy theories? Use this site
to generate your own.
http://www.westword.com/extra/conspire.html

A final site

FinalThoughts.com
The Website where you can plan the end of your life.
http://www.FinalThoughts.com

index